THE AUSTRALIAN
Women's Weekly

The length of time I've worked in the food industry hasn't dampened my enthusiasm for cooking in the slightest... the trouble is finding the hours to indulge in my favourite form of relaxation. The fact that I find it fun (as I've discovered many of my friends and readers do) to spend a few hours during the weekend creating and "playing" in my kitchen while at the same time preparing a special family meal, evolved into *The Weekend Cook,* a book to turn to any day of the week, whenever you feel like cooking just for the pleasure of it.

Pamela Clark
Food Director

contents

harira

PREPARATION TIME 25 MINUTES (PLUS STANDING TIME) **COOKING TIME** 2 HOURS 15 MINUTES

After sundown during Ramadan, many of the Muslims in Morocco and other North African countries break the day's fast by starting their meal with this hearty soup. Recipes vary from family to family but chickpeas and lamb always feature as constant ingredients.

1 cup (200g) dried chickpeas
20g butter
2 medium brown onions (300g),
   chopped finely
2 trimmed celery stalks (200g),
   chopped finely
2 cloves garlic, crushed
4cm piece fresh ginger
   (20g), grated
1 teaspoon ground cinnamon
½ teaspoon ground black pepper
pinch saffron threads
500g diced lamb
3 large tomatoes (750g), seeded,
   chopped coarsely
2 litres (8 cups) hot water
½ cup (100g) brown lentils
2 tablespoons plain flour
½ cup (100g) white long-grain rice
½ cup firmly packed fresh
   coriander leaves
2 tablespoons lemon juice

1 Place chickpeas in medium bowl, cover with water; stand overnight, drain. Rinse under cold water; drain.

2 Heat butter in large saucepan; cook onion, celery and garlic, stirring, until onion softens. Add ginger, cinnamon, pepper and saffron; cook, stirring, about 2 minutes or until fragrant. Add lamb; cook, stirring, about 5 minutes or until lamb is browned.

3 Add chickpeas and tomato; cook, stirring, about 5 minutes or until tomato softens.

4 Stir in the water; bring to a boil. Reduce heat; simmer, covered, 45 minutes. Add lentils; simmer, covered, 1 hour.

5 Blend flour with ½ cup of the slightly cooled cooking liquid in small bowl; stir into lamb mixture with rice. Cook, stirring, until mixture boils and thickens. (Can be made ahead to this stage. Cover; refrigerate overnight.) Stir coriander and juice into harira just before serving. If desired, garnish each bowl with extra coriander leaves.

serves 8
per serving 13.4g fat; 1364kJ (326 cal)

thai chicken broth with coriander wontons

PREPARATION TIME 40 MINUTES (PLUS REFRIGERATION TIME) **COOKING TIME** 2 HOURS 50 MINUTES

We suggest you make the broth either the day before or in the morning on the day you want to eat this delectable, clean-tasting soup so that it can chill long enough for the fat to solidify on top; scoop it off and discard it for a beautifully clear stock. Chicken shops generally sell raw carcasses in 1kg packages; you need 2kg of chicken bones for this recipe.

4 litres (16 cups) water

2kg chicken bones

2 medium brown onions (300g), chopped coarsely

2 stalks fresh lemon grass, chopped coarsely

4cm piece fresh ginger (20g), chopped coarsely

2 fresh long red chillies, halved crossways

2 cloves garlic, quartered

1 teaspoon black peppercorns

300g chicken mince

2 teaspoons finely chopped fresh coriander

1 clove garlic, crushed

2cm piece fresh ginger (10g), grated

1 fresh red thai chilli, seeded, chopped finely

¼ cup (60ml) soy sauce

30 wonton wrappers

1 egg white

1 tablespoon lime juice

1 tablespoon mirin

1 cup watercress sprigs

3 green onions, sliced thinly

2 fresh long red chillies, seeded, sliced thinly

⅓ cup loosely packed fresh coriander leaves

1 Combine the water, chicken bones, brown onion, lemon grass, chopped ginger, halved chilli, quartered garlic and peppercorns in large saucepan; bring to a boil. Reduce heat; simmer, uncovered, 2½ hours. Strain broth through muslin-lined sieve or colander into large bowl; discard solids. Allow broth to cool, cover; refrigerate until cold. (Can be made ahead to this stage. Cover; refrigerate overnight.)

2 Combine chicken mince in medium bowl with chopped coriander, crushed garlic, grated ginger, chopped chilli and 1 tablespoon of the soy sauce. Place 1 rounded teaspoon of the chicken mixture in centre of each wrapper; brush around edges with egg white, gather edges around filling, pinch together to seal. Repeat process with remaining wrappers and filling.

3 Skim fat from surface of broth; return broth to large saucepan, bring to a boil. Cook wontons, in two batches, about 4 minutes or until cooked through. Using slotted spoon, transfer wontons from pan to individual serving bowls. Stir remaining soy sauce, juice and mirin into broth; return to a boil. Top wontons with watercress, green onion, sliced chilli and coriander leaves; ladle broth into bowls.

serves 6

per serving 4.7g fat; 691kJ (165 cal)

tip Uncooked wontons can be frozen, covered, for up to 3 months; they can be cooked in the broth straight from the freezer.

cuban black bean soup

PREPARATION TIME 30 MINUTES (PLUS STANDING TIME) **COOKING TIME** 2 HOURS 15 MINUTES

Black beans, also known as turtle beans, are a common ingredient in Caribbean and Latin American soups, salsas and salads. They are available from health food stores and gourmet food outlets, but are not the same as chinese black beans, which are fermented soy beans. Ask your butcher to cut the ham bone in half for you so it fits more easily into the pan.

2½ cups (500g) dried black beans
1kg ham bone
¼ cup (60ml) olive oil
2 medium brown onions (300g),
    chopped finely
1 medium red capsicum (200g),
    chopped finely
4 cloves garlic, crushed
1 tablespoon ground cumin
1 teaspoon dried chilli flakes
400g can chopped tomatoes
2.5 litres (10 cups) water
1 tablespoon dried oregano
2 teaspoons ground black pepper
¼ cup (60ml) lime juice
2 medium tomatoes (300g),
    chopped finely
¼ cup coarsely chopped
    fresh coriander

1 Place beans in medium bowl, cover with water; stand overnight, drain. Rinse under cold water; drain.

2 Preheat oven to hot; roast ham bone on oven tray, uncovered, 30 minutes.

3 Meanwhile, heat oil in large saucepan; cook onion, capsicum and garlic, stirring, about 5 minutes or until vegetables soften. Add cumin and chilli; cook, stirring, 1 minute. Add beans and ham bone to pan with undrained tomatoes, the water, oregano and pepper; bring to a boil. Reduce heat; simmer, uncovered, 1½ hours. (Can be made ahead to this stage. Cover; refrigerate overnight.)

4 Remove ham bone from soup; shred ham from bone. Discard bone; add ham to soup, stirring until heated through. Stir juice, tomato and coriander into soup just before serving.

serves 8

per serving 7.3g fat; 650kJ (155 cal)

tip Some Cuban recipes call for half of the beans to be mashed then returned to the soup, giving it a smoother, almost velvet-like consistency.

serving suggestion Traditionally, a tureen of black bean soup is surrounded on the table by small bowls of various complementary condiments such as chopped hard-boiled egg; sour cream or crème fraîche; paper-thin wedges of lime; finely chopped red onion; finely chopped chillies in red wine vinegar; and more fresh chopped tomato and coriander leaves. The diners help themselves to whatever flavours they prefer stirred into their individual bowl of soup.

borscht

PREPARATION TIME I HOUR 30 MINUTES (PLUS REFRIGERATION TIME) COOKING TIME 5 HOURS 50 MINUTES

Perhaps the most famous of Russian soups, borscht can be served hot or cold, pureed or chunky, meatless or made with shredded beef. When the Ukraine was the beet-growing centre of the Russias in centuries past, this soup became a traditional part of the region's daily diet. Make the beef stock either the day before or in the morning of the day you want to eat this satisfying soup so that it can chill long enough for the fat to solidify on top; scoop it away before reheating the stock.

1kg beef bones (shin or shank, cut into pieces)

3 medium brown onions (450g), unpeeled, quartered

6 litres (24 cups) water

2 trimmed celery stalks (200g), chopped coarsely

2 medium carrots (240g), chopped coarsely

2 bay leaves

1 teaspoon black peppercorns

20g butter

1 large brown onion (200g), chopped finely

2 medium carrots (240g), chopped finely

1 medium leek (350g), chopped finely

3 trimmed celery stalks (300g), chopped finely

3 bacon rashers (200g), rind removed, chopped finely

5 medium beetroots (1.5kg), peeled, chopped finely

3 medium tomatoes (450g), peeled, chopped finely

¼ small cabbage (300g), shredded finely

300g sour cream

1 tablespoon finely chopped fresh dill

1 Preheat oven to hot; roast bones and unpeeled onion on oven tray, uncovered, about 1 hour or until browned.

2 Combine bones and onion with the water, coarsely chopped celery and carrot, bay leaves and peppercorns in large saucepan or boiler; bring to a boil. Reduce heat; simmer, uncovered, 3½ hours. Strain stock through muslin-lined sieve or colander into large bowl; discard solids. Allow stock to cool, cover; refrigerate until cold. (Can be made ahead to this stage. Cover; refrigerate overnight.)

3 Heat butter in large saucepan; cook finely chopped onion, carrot, leek, finely chopped celery and bacon, stirring, until vegetables just soften. Discard fat from surface of stock. Add stock to pan with beetroot, tomato and cabbage; bring to a boil. Reduce heat; simmer, uncovered, 1 hour.

4 Blend or process (or pass through a food mill [mouli] or fine sieve) half of the borscht, in batches, until smooth, then return to pan. Reheat until hot, then divide borscht among serving bowls; dollop combined sour cream and dill into each bowl.

serves 6
per serving 25g fat; 1692kJ (404 cal)

mezze platter

Spell it however you like – mezze, meze, mezza – at the end of the day it translates from Arabic as a group of appetisers traditionally served as an entrée but sometimes comprising the entire meal. Here is a selection of seven mezze recipes which, presented together on individual plates, will serve eight diners as a main course. Accompany the mezze with warmed pitta, torn into pieces. The recipes that comprise this mezze are shown below in the order we suggest you make them: for instance, the pickled cauliflower should be prepared and stood at least 3 days before it is eaten so it should be the recipe you turn to first.

pickled cauliflower

PREPARATION TIME 15 MINUTES COOKING TIME 5 MINUTES

3 cups (750ml) water
1½ cups (375ml) white
    wine vinegar
¼ cup (55g) table salt
½ small cauliflower (500g),
    cut into florets
1 medium white turnip (230g),
    cut into 1cm wedges
8 baby beetroots (200g),
    unpeeled, cut into wedges
1 clove garlic, sliced thinly

1 Combine the water, vinegar and salt in medium saucepan; bring to a boil. Boil, uncovered, for 3 minutes.
2 Pack vegetables and garlic into hot sterilised 1.5-litre (6-cup) glass jar with tight-fitting lid; pour in enough boiling vinegar mixture to leave 1cm space between vegetable pieces and top of jar. Seal while hot. Store in cool, dark place for at least 3 days before eating; once opened, store jar in refrigerator.

makes 4½ cups
per ¼ cup 0.1g fat; 58kJ (14 cal)

Mezze platter, clockwise from left:
pickled cauliflower; lahma bi ajeen;
spinach fillo triangles; baba ghanoush;
tabbouleh; hummus; labne.

lahma bi ajeen (mini lamb pies)

PREPARATION TIME 30 MINUTES (PLUS STANDING TIME) COOKING TIME 10 MINUTES

1 cup (150g) plain flour
1 teaspoon (4g) dry yeast
½ teaspoon sea salt flakes
1 tablespoon olive oil
½ cup (125ml) warm water
olive-oil spray

SPICED LAMB TOPPING
100g lamb mince
1 medium tomato (150g),
    chopped finely
1 teaspoon ground cumin
1 teaspoon ground coriander
1 tablespoon finely chopped
    fresh coriander
2 teaspoons toasted pine nuts,
    chopped coarsely

1 Process flour, yeast, salt, oil and enough of the warm water until mixture forms a ball. Place ball of dough in oiled medium bowl; spray dough with oil. Cover; stand in warm place about 1 hour or until dough doubles in size.
2 Meanwhile, make spiced lamb topping. Preheat oven to moderately hot.
3 Knead dough on lightly floured surface 5 minutes; roll dough to 2mm thickness. Using 7cm cutter, cut 20 rounds from dough; place rounds on oiled oven tray.
4 Divide topping among rounds, spreading to edge to completely cover round. Bake, uncovered, in moderately hot oven about 10 minutes or until lahma bi ajeen are cooked through.

SPICED LAMB TOPPING Combine ingredients in small bowl.

makes 20
per piece 2.1g fat; 205kJ (49 cal)

spinach fillo triangles
PREPARATION TIME 45 MINUTES COOKING TIME 15 MINUTES

400g spinach, trimmed,
  shredded finely
2 teaspoons sumac
2 green onions, chopped finely
1 tablespoon lemon juice
4 sheets fillo pastry
olive-oil spray

1 Preheat oven to moderately hot. Oil oven tray.
2 Boil, steam or microwave spinach until wilted; drain, squeeze out as
   much excess liquid as possible. Combine spinach in small bowl with
   sumac, onion and juice.
3 Cut each pastry sheet lengthways into four strips. Place one strip on
   board; cover remaining strips with baking paper, then with damp tea towel.
4 Spray strip with oil; place 1 rounded teaspoon of spinach filling on one
   corner, 5mm from edge, flatten slightly. Fold opposite corner of strip
   diagonally across filling to form triangle; continue folding to end of strip,
   retaining triangular shape. Place fillo triangle on prepared tray, seam-side
   down; repeat process with remaining strips and filling.
5 Spray tops of fillo triangles lightly with oil; bake, uncovered, in moderately
   hot oven about 10 minutes or until just crisp and browned lightly.

makes 16
per piece 3.1g fat; 163kJ (39 cal)

labne

PREPARATION TIME 20 MINUTES (PLUS REFRIGERATION TIME)

This recipe must be prepared at least 2 days before
you want to serve the mezze.

3 cups (840g) greek-style yogurt
3 teaspoons salt
¼ cup (60ml) olive oil

1 Combine yogurt and salt in medium bowl; pour into muslin-lined large
sieve or colander set over large bowl. Gather corners of muslin together,
twist, then tie with kitchen string. Place heavy can on muslin to weight
yogurt mixture; refrigerate 24 to 36 hours until yogurt thickens (yogurt
will lose about half its weight in water; discard water in bowl).
2 Place thickened yogurt in small bowl; discard muslin. Roll level
tablespoons of yogurt into balls; place balls on platter, drizzle with oil.

makes 24 balls
per ball 4.7g fat; 264kJ (63 cal)
tip Labne will keep for up to 2 months in the refrigerator; pack balls
into clean glass jar with tight-fitting lid, cover with olive oil, seal jar tightly
before refrigerating.

hummus

PREPARATION TIME 10 MINUTES COOKING TIME 15 MINUTES

2 cups (500ml) water
2 x 300g cans chickpeas, rinsed, drained
¼ cup (60ml) lemon juice
¼ cup (60ml) olive oil
⅓ cup (80ml) tahini
3 cloves garlic, crushed
1 tablespoon olive oil, extra

1 Place the water and chickpeas in medium saucepan; bring to a boil. Boil,
uncovered, about 10 minutes or until beans are tender. Strain chickpeas
over medium bowl; reserve 1 cup cooking liquid.
2 Blend or process chickpeas and reserved cooking liquid with juice, oil,
tahini and garlic until just smooth.
3 Drizzle hummus with extra oil.

makes 2 cups
per ¼ cup 16.3g fat; 814kJ (195 cal)

baba ghanoush

PREPARATION TIME 15 MINUTES (PLUS STANDING TIME)
COOKING TIME 30 MINUTES

2 large eggplants (1kg)
3 cloves garlic, crushed
2 tablespoons tahini
¼ cup (60ml) lemon juice
2 tablespoons olive oil
½ teaspoon sweet paprika

1 Pierce eggplants all over with fork or skewer; place, on oiled oven tray, under preheated grill about 30 minutes or until skin blackens and eggplant is soft, turning occasionally. Stand 15 minutes.
2 Peel eggplants, discard skin; drain eggplants in colander 10 minutes, then blend or process with remaining ingredients.

makes 2 cups
per ¼ cup 7.9g fat; 385kJ (92 cal)

tabbouleh

PREPARATION TIME 30 MINUTES (PLUS REFRIGERATION TIME)

¼ cup (40g) burghul
3 medium tomatoes (450g)
3 cups coarsely chopped fresh flat-leaf parsley
2 green onions, chopped finely
¼ cup finely chopped fresh mint
¼ cup (60ml) lemon juice
¼ cup (60ml) extra virgin olive oil

1 Place burghul in small shallow bowl. Halve tomatoes; using small spoon, scoop pulp from tomato halves over burghul. Chop remaining tomato flesh finely; spread over burghul so surface is completely covered with tomato. Cover bowl; refrigerate 1 hour.
2 Place burghul mixture in large bowl with remaining ingredients; toss tabbouleh gently to combine.

makes 4½ cups
per ¼ cup 3.1g fat; 164kJ (39 cal)
tip Chop the mint just before assembling the tabbouleh in the bowl because it has a tendency to blacken and go limp after it's cut.

roasted vegetable parcels with tapenade dressing

PREPARATION TIME 30 MINUTES **COOKING TIME** 30 MINUTES

There are two products sold as rice paper: the one used in this recipe, Vietnamese in origin, is made from rice paste that's been stamped into rounds and can be kept at room temperature. Dipped briefly in water, these rounds become pliable wrappers for deep-fried or uncooked foods, most often vegetables. The other, called glossy rice paper and generally imported from Holland, is whiter than the other and looks like a grainy sheet of paper. It is used in confectionery making and baking.

¼ cup (60ml) olive oil
1 medium red onion (170g),
    sliced thickly
3 baby eggplants (180g), halved
    lengthways, chopped coarsely
2 medium zucchini (240g), halved
    lengthways, chopped coarsely
200g mushrooms, quartered
1 clove garlic, crushed
2 tablespoons balsamic vinegar
250g cherry tomatoes
6 thin slices pancetta (90g)
6 x 22cm rice paper rounds
150g piece goat cheese,
    cut into 6 even slices
6 sprigs fresh flat-leaf parsley

TAPENADE DRESSING
½ cup (75g) seeded
    kalamata olives
2 teaspoons drained baby
    capers, rinsed
3 drained anchovy fillets
2 tablespoons coarsely chopped
    fresh flat-leaf parsley
2 teaspoons lemon juice
¼ cup (60ml) olive oil
2 tablespoons hot water

1 Preheat oven to very hot. Reserve 1 teaspoon of the olive oil; combine remaining oil in large shallow baking dish with onion, eggplant, zucchini and mushrooms. Roast, uncovered, in very hot oven, tossing occasionally, about 15 minutes or until vegetables are browned lightly. Add garlic, vinegar and tomatoes; toss to combine. Roast, uncovered, 10 minutes; remove from oven. Cool 10 minutes.

2 Meanwhile, make tapenade dressing.

3 Heat reserved oil in medium frying pan; cook pancetta, uncovered, until crisp both sides. Drain on absorbent paper.

4 Place one rice paper round in medium bowl of warm water until just softened; lift sheet carefully from water, place on tea-towel-covered board. Centre a sixth of the vegetable mixture on round; to enclose filling, fold in all four sides, overlapping slightly to form a square shape. Place parcel on baking-paper-lined oven tray, seam-side down; top each with cheese slice. Repeat process with remaining rounds, vegetable mixture and cheese.

5 Cook under preheated grill about 2 minutes or until cheese just browns and parcels are heated through. Place parcels on serving plates; drizzle with tapenade dressing, top with parsley then pancetta.

TAPENADE DRESSING Blend or process ingredients until mixture forms a coarse paste.

serves 6
per serving 24.9g fat; 1248kJ (298 cal)
tip Tapenade dressing can be made up to 3 days ahead; keep, covered, under refrigeration.

cheese and crepe soufflés

PREPARATION TIME 20 MINUTES (PLUS STANDING TIME) **COOKING TIME** 50 MINUTES

You'll need to buy 50g pieces of both the gruyère and the parmesan for this recipe.

⅓ cup (50g) plain flour

1 egg

1 egg yolk

20g butter, melted

½ cup (125ml) milk

1 tablespoon finely chopped fresh
    garlic chives

1 large red capsicum (350g)

1 clove garlic, crushed

½ cup (125ml) cream

CHEESE SOUFFLÉ

30g butter

2 tablespoons plain flour

1 cup (250ml) milk

4 eggs, separated

¼ cup (30g) finely grated
    gruyère cheese

¼ cup (20g) finely grated
    parmesan cheese

¼ teaspoon cayenne pepper

1 Place flour in small bowl; make well in centre. Gradually whisk in combined egg and yolk, butter and milk; strain batter into small jug. Stir in chives, cover; stand crepe batter 30 minutes.

2 Meanwhile, quarter capsicum, remove and discard seeds and membranes. Roast under preheated grill or in very hot oven, skin-side up, until skin blisters and blackens. Cover capsicum pieces with plastic or paper for 5 minutes, peel away skin; chop coarsely. Blend or process capsicum with garlic and cream until mixture is smooth. Pour into small saucepan; stand at room temperature while making soufflés.

3 Heat oiled crepe pan or 20cm heavy-based non-stick frying pan; pour about 2 tablespoons of the batter into pan, tilting pan so batter coats base evenly. Cook over low heat, loosening edge with spatula until crepe is browned lightly. Turn crepe; cook until browned on other side. Turn crepe onto wire rack; repeat process with remaining batter to make six crepes in total.

4 Preheat oven to moderately hot. Make cheese soufflé.

5 Lightly grease six ¾-cup (180ml) soufflé dishes; place on oven tray. Gently push one crepe into each of the soufflé dishes to line base and side. Divide soufflé mixture among crepe "cases"; bake, uncovered, in moderately hot oven about 20 minutes or until browned lightly. Working quickly, carefully turn soufflés onto serving plates; turn top-side up, drizzle with reheated capsicum sauce. Serve immediately.

CHEESE SOUFFLÉ Melt butter in small saucepan, add flour; cook, stirring, about 1 minute or until mixture thickens and bubbles. Gradually stir in milk; bring to a boil, stirring until sauce boils and thickens. Transfer mixture to large bowl, stir in egg yolks, cheeses and pepper; cool 5 minutes. Meanwhile, beat egg whites in small bowl with electric mixer until soft peaks form. Gently fold whites into cheese mixture, in two batches, until just combined.

serves 6
per serving 25.2g fat; 1407kJ (336 cal)
tip Crepes can be made up to 1 day ahead and kept, covered, under refrigeration until required.

pumpkin and eggplant laksa

PREPARATION TIME 45 MINUTES **COOKING TIME** 20 MINUTES

Keep the roots from the bunch of fresh coriander you buy for this recipe because they are used, cleaned and chopped, in the laksa paste.

½ cup (125g) laksa paste (see
    recipe below)
700g piece butternut pumpkin,
    diced into 2cm pieces
5 baby eggplants (300g),
    sliced thickly
3 cups (750ml) vegetable stock
1⅔ cups (400ml) coconut milk
250g rice stick noodles
500g bok choy, chopped coarsely
2 tablespoons lime juice
1¼ cups (100g) bean sprouts
6 green onions, sliced thinly
½ cup loosely packed fresh
    coriander leaves
½ cup loosely packed fresh
    vietnamese mint leaves

LAKSA PASTE
7 dried medium red chillies
½ cup (125ml) boiling water
1 tablespoon peanut oil
3 cloves garlic, quartered
1 medium brown onion (150g),
    chopped coarsely
1 stick fresh lemon grass,
    trimmed, chopped finely
4cm piece fresh ginger
    (20g), grated
1 tablespoon halved
    macadamias (10g)
roots from 1 bunch coriander,
    washed, chopped coarsely
1 teaspoon ground turmeric
1 teaspoon ground coriander
2 teaspoons salt
¼ cup loosely packed fresh
    vietnamese mint leaves

1 Make laksa paste. Place ½ cup of the paste in large saucepan; cook, stirring, about 1 minute or until fragrant. Add pumpkin and eggplant; cook, stirring, 2 minutes. Add stock and coconut milk; bring to a boil. Reduce heat; simmer laksa mixture, covered, about 10 minutes or until vegetables are just tender.

2 Meanwhile, place noodles in large heatproof bowl, cover with boiling water, stand until just tender; drain.

3 Stir bok choy into laksa; return to a boil. Stir juice into laksa off the heat. Divide noodles among serving bowls; ladle laksa over noodles, sprinkle with combined sprouts, onion and herbs.

LAKSA PASTE Cover chillies with the boiling water in small heatproof bowl; stand 10 minutes, drain. Blend or process chillies with remaining ingredients until mixture forms a smooth paste. Measure ½ cup of the paste for this recipe, then freeze the remainder, covered, for future use.

serves 6
per serving 17.5g fat; 1521kJ; (363 cal)

minestrone alla milanese

PREPARATION TIME 40 MINUTES (PLUS STANDING AND REFRIGERATION TIMES) **COOKING TIME** 3 HOURS 35 MINUTES

There are as many versions of minestrone as there are regions in Italy, and this recipe is based on a seasonal soup made in Milan, capital of the northern region of Lombardy, where the colder winters seem to inspire hearty fare like this. Rice, rather than pasta or bread, is used as a thickener, and the ham hocks impart a pleasing smoky flavour that seems to fight the chill.

⅔ cup (130g) dried borlotti beans

2 ham hocks (1kg)

1 medium brown onion (150g), chopped coarsely

1 trimmed celery stalk (100g), chopped coarsely

1 teaspoon black peppercorns

1 bay leaf

3 medium carrots (360g), chopped coarsely

4 litres (16 cups) water

1 tablespoon olive oil

1 large white onion (200g), chopped coarsely

3 cloves garlic, crushed

4 small tomatoes (360g), peeled, chopped coarsely

1 tablespoon tomato paste

2 trimmed celery stalks (200g), chopped coarsely, extra

2 medium potatoes (400g), chopped coarsely

½ small cabbage (600g), shredded coarsely

2 medium zucchini (240g), chopped coarsely

½ cup (100g) arborio rice

¼ cup finely chopped fresh flat-leaf parsley

2 tablespoons finely shredded fresh basil leaves

1 Place beans in medium bowl, cover with water; stand overnight, drain. Rinse under cold water; drain.

2 Preheat oven to hot; roast ham hocks and onion on oven tray, uncovered, 30 minutes. Combine ham hocks and onion with celery, peppercorns, bay leaf, a third of the carrot and the water in large saucepan; bring to a boil. Reduce heat; simmer, uncovered, 2 hours. Strain stock through muslin-lined sieve or colander into large bowl; discard solids. Allow stock to cool, cover; refrigerate until cold. (Can be made ahead to this stage. Cover; refrigerate overnight.)

3 Heat oil in large saucepan; cook onion and garlic, stirring, until onion softens. Discard fat from surface of stock. Add stock, beans and tomato to pan with tomato paste, extra celery, potato and remaining carrot; bring to a boil. Reduce heat; simmer, covered, about 40 minutes or until beans are just tender.

4 Add cabbage, zucchini and rice; simmer, uncovered, about 15 minutes or until rice is just tender. Stir in parsley and basil just before serving.

serves 6

per serving 3.6g fat; 790kJ (189 cal)

tip You can substitute a small short pasta such as pennette, conchigliette (baby shells) or even elbow macaroni for the rice if you prefer; add it with the cabbage and zucchini, but cook it only until al dente.

Slide knife under top of shell at back of each crab, lever off shell.

Discard whitish gills from crabs, then rinse well under cold water.

Peel the cored tomatoes, pulling from cross in base towards top.

bouillabaisse with aïoli and rouille

PREPARATION TIME 1 HOUR 15 MINUTES COOKING TIME 40 MINUTES

Aïoli is an addictive garlic mayonnaise that has inflamed the passions of so many people around the world that local aïoli festivals are held at garlic harvest time every year. French for "rust", rouille is a capsicum- and chilli-flavoured mayonnaise-like sauce often used to garnish seafood stews.

700g uncooked large prawns
2 uncooked medium blue
    swimmer crabs (650g)
10 small tomatoes (900g)
1 tablespoon olive oil
1 clove garlic, crushed
1 large brown onion (200g),
    chopped coarsely
1 medium leek (350g),
    chopped coarsely
1 untrimmed tiny fennel (130g),
    chopped coarsely
1 fresh red thai chilli, seeded,
    chopped coarsely
1 bay leaf
pinch saffron threads
10cm piece fresh orange peel
1.5 litres (6 cups) water
1 cup (250ml) dry white wine
750g firm white fish fillets,
    chopped coarsely
500g small black mussels
½ cup coarsely chopped fresh
    flat-leaf parsley
1 long french bread stick

AÏOLI
3 cloves garlic, quartered
2 egg yolks
2 tablespoons lemon juice
½ teaspoon dijon mustard
⅔ cup (160ml) olive oil

ROUILLE
1 medium red capsicum (200g)
1 fresh red thai chilli, seeded,
    chopped finely
1 clove garlic, quartered
1 cup (70g) stale breadcrumbs
1 tablespoon lemon juice
¼ cup (60ml) olive oil

1 Shell and devein prawns, leaving tails intact. Reserve heads and shells; place prawn meat in medium bowl. Slide knife under top of crab shell at back, lever off; reserve with prawn shells. Discard gills; rinse crabs under cold water. Cut crab bodies into quarters; place in bowl with prawn meat.

2 Chop four of the tomatoes coarsely; reserve with seafood shells.

3 Core then cut shallow cross in base of remaining tomatoes, place in large heatproof bowl; cover with boiling water. Stand 2 minutes; drain then peel, from cross end towards top. Quarter tomatoes; scoop out seeds, reserve with seafood shells. Chop tomato flesh finely; reserve.

4 Heat oil in large saucepan; cook reserved seafood shell mixture with the coarsely chopped tomato, garlic, onion, leek, fennel, chilli, bay leaf, saffron and peel, stirring, about 10 minutes or until shells change in colour and vegetables soften. Add the water and wine, cover; bring to a boil. Reduce heat; simmer, covered, 10 minutes. Remove crab shells.

5 Blend or process seafood mixture (including prawn shells), in batches, until smooth; using wooden spoon, push each batch through large sieve into large saucepan. Discard solids in sieve. Reserve ¼ cup strained seafood mixture for rouille (see below). (Can be made ahead to this stage. Cover; refrigerate overnight.)

6 Make aïoli and rouille.

7 Add finely chopped tomatoes to strained seafood mixture; bring to a boil. Add fish and mussels, return to a boil; cook, covered, 5 minutes. Add reserved prawn meat and crab pieces; cook, covered, 5 minutes. Stir parsley into bouillabaisse; serve with sliced toasted bread, aïoli and rouille.

AÏOLI Blend or process garlic, yolks, juice and mustard until smooth. With motor operating, gradually add oil in steady stream; process until aïoli thickens. (Can be made a day ahead. Cover; refrigerate overnight.)
ROUILLE Quarter capsicum; discard seeds and membrane. Roast under preheated grill or in very hot oven, skin-side up, until skin blackens. Cover capsicum pieces in plastic or paper for 5 minutes; peel away skin, then chop coarsely. Blend or process capsicum with chilli, garlic, breadcrumbs, juice and reserved ¼ cup strained seafood mixture liquid until smooth. With motor operating, gradually add oil in thin, steady stream; process until rouille thickens. (Can be made a day ahead. Cover; refrigerate overnight.)

serves 6
per serving 58.2g fat; 3878kJ (926 cal)

lamb shank stew with creamy mash

PREPARATION TIME 20 MINUTES **COOKING TIME** 3 HOURS 20 MINUTES

To "french" a lamb shank (or rack or cutlet) means to clean away excess gristle, fat and meat from the end of the shank (or cutlet or rack), thus exposing the bone. Trimmed shanks look somewhat like giant chicken legs and, indeed, some butchers do call them "lamb drumsticks".

8 french-trimmed lamb
   shanks (1.6kg)
8 cloves garlic, halved
2 medium lemons (280g)
2 tablespoons olive oil
3 large brown onions (600g),
   chopped coarsely
2 cups (500ml) dry red wine
3 medium carrots (360g),
   quartered lengthways
3 trimmed celery stalks (300g),
   chopped coarsely
4 bay leaves
8 sprigs fresh thyme
1.75 litres (7 cups) chicken stock
½ cup finely chopped fresh
   flat-leaf parsley
¼ cup finely chopped fresh mint
2kg potatoes, chopped coarsely
300ml cream
100g butter

1 Pierce meatiest part of each shank in two places with sharp knife; press garlic into cuts.

2 Grate rind of both lemons finely; reserve. Halve lemons; rub cut sides all over shanks. Preheat oven to moderate.

3 Heat oil in large flameproof casserole dish; cook shanks, in batches, until browned. Cook onion, stirring, in same dish until softened. Add wine; bring to a boil, then remove dish from heat.

4 Place carrot, celery and shanks, in alternate layers, on onion mixture in dish. Top with bay leaves and thyme; carefully pour stock over the top. Cover dish tightly with lid or foil; cook in moderate oven about 3 hours or until meat is tender. (Can be made ahead to this stage. Cover; refrigerate overnight.)

5 Meanwhile, combine reserved grated rind, parsley and mint in small bowl.

6 Boil, steam or microwave potato until tender; drain. Mash potato with warmed cream and butter in large bowl until smooth. Cover to keep warm.

7 Transfer shanks to platter; cover to keep warm. Strain pan juices through muslin-lined sieve or colander into medium saucepan; discard solids. Boil pan juices, uncovered, stirring occasionally, until reduced by half.

8 Divide mashed potato among serving plates; top with shanks, sprinkle with lemon-herb mixture, drizzle with pan juices. Serve with steamed green beans, if desired.

serves 8
per serving 39.8g fat; 2856kJ (682 cal)

dhansak with caramelised onion brown rice

PREPARATION TIME I HOUR 15 MINUTES (PLUS STANDING TIME) **COOKING TIME** I HOUR 40 MINUTES

Dhansak, a lentil and meat stew, is a tantalisingly complex mixture of traditional Persian and Indian food elements. It is always served with "brown" rice – white rice cooked with caramelised onion until it changes colour.

1 cup (200g) yellow split peas
½ cup (100g) dried chickpeas
½ cup (100g) red lentils
⅓ cup (80ml) vegetable oil
1kg diced lamb
1 large eggplant (500g), chopped coarsely
800g pumpkin, chopped coarsely
5 medium tomatoes (750g), peeled, chopped coarsely
1kg medium brown onions, sliced thinly

GARAM MASALA

1 tablespoon ground coriander
2 teaspoons ground cumin
2 teaspoons ground turmeric
½ teaspoon ground cinnamon
½ teaspoon ground cardamom
½ teaspoon black mustard seeds
¼ teaspoon ground clove

MASALA PASTE

6 dried small red chillies
6 long green chillies, seeded
4cm piece fresh ginger (20g), chopped coarsely
6 cloves garlic, quartered
½ cup firmly packed fresh mint leaves
½ cup firmly packed fresh coriander leaves
¼ cup (60ml) hot water

CARAMELISED ONION BROWN RICE

2½ cups (500g) basmati rice
1.25 litres (5 cups) water
2 tablespoons vegetable oil
20g butter
4 medium brown onions (600g), sliced thinly

1 Place split peas and chickpeas in large bowl, cover with water; stand overnight, drain. Rinse under cold water; drain. Rinse lentils under cold water; drain. Combine lentils, split peas and chickpeas in large saucepan of boiling water; return to a boil. Reduce heat; simmer, uncovered, about 40 minutes or until chickpeas are tender.

2 Meanwhile, make garam masala and masala paste. Heat half of the oil in large frying pan; cook lamb, in batches, until just browned. Reserve.

3 Drain pea mixture through sieve over large bowl. Return 1 litre cooking liquid to same pan, discard remainder. Reserve pea mixture in same bowl.

4 Place eggplant, pumpkin, tomato and about a third of the sliced onion in pan with reserved cooking liquid, cover; bring to a boil. Reduce heat; simmer dhansak, covered, 10 minutes, stirring occasionally. Drain vegetable mixture through sieve over another large bowl; reserve 2 cups of the cooking liquid, discard remainder.

5 Combine half of the split pea mixture and half of the vegetable mixture in large bowl; mash until smooth.

6 Heat same cleaned pan; dry-fry garam masala and masala paste, stirring, until fragrant. Add mashed and whole split pea and vegetable mixtures, lamb and reserved cooking liquid to pan; bring to a boil. Reduce heat; simmer, uncovered, 45 minutes, stirring occasionally. (Can be made ahead to this stage. Cover; refrigerate overnight or freeze.)

7 Meanwhile, make caramelised onion brown rice.

8 Heat remaining oil in large frying pan; cook remaining sliced onion, stirring, about 15 minutes or until softened and caramelised lightly. Sprinkle onion over dhansak; serve with rice, and lemon wedges, if desired.

GARAM MASALA Combine all ingredients in small bowl.
MASALA PASTE Blend or process ingredients until mixture forms a smooth paste.
CARAMELISED ONION BROWN RICE Wash rice in strainer under cold water until water runs clear; drain. Heat oil and butter in medium saucepan; cook onion, stirring, about 15 minutes or until softened and lightly caramelised. Carefully add the water to pan; bring to a boil. Stir in rice; return to a boil. Reduce heat; simmer rice, partially covered, about 10 minutes or until steam holes appear on the surface. Cover rice tightly, reduce heat to as low as possible; steam 10 minutes (do not remove lid). Remove from heat; stand 10 minutes without removing lid. Fluff with fork before serving.

serves 8
per serving 37.4g fat; 3653kJ (873 cal)

chicken, olive and lemon tagine

PREPARATION TIME 30 MINUTES (PLUS STANDING TIME) **COOKING TIME** 2 HOURS 30 MINUTES

1 cup (200g) dried chickpeas

2 tablespoons plain flour

2 teaspoons hot paprika

8 chicken drumsticks (1.2kg)

8 chicken thigh cutlets (1.3kg)

40g butter

2 medium red onions (340g),
  sliced thickly

3 cloves garlic, crushed

1 teaspoon cumin seeds

½ teaspoon ground turmeric

½ teaspoon ground coriander

¼ teaspoon saffron threads

1 teaspoon dried chilli flakes

1 teaspoon ground ginger

3 cups (750ml) chicken stock

2 tablespoons finely sliced
  preserved lemon rind

⅓ cup (40g) seeded green olives

2 tablespoons finely chopped
  fresh coriander

TUNISIAN-STYLE RICE

3 cups (600g) white long-grain rice

20g butter

1.5 litres (6 cups) water

1 Place chickpeas in medium bowl, cover with water; stand overnight, drain. Rinse under cold water; drain. Place chickpeas in medium saucepan of boiling water; return to a boil. Reduce heat; simmer, uncovered, about 40 minutes or until chickpeas are tender.

2 Preheat oven to moderately slow.

3 Place flour and paprika in paper or plastic bag, add chicken pieces, in batches; shake gently to coat chicken in flour mixture.

4 Melt butter in large flameproof casserole dish; cook chicken pieces, in batches, until browned. Cook onion in same dish, stirring, until softened. Add garlic, cumin, turmeric, ground coriander, saffron, chilli and ginger; cook, stirring, until fragrant. Return chicken with stock to dish; bring to a boil, then cook, covered, in moderately slow oven 30 minutes. Add drained chickpeas; cook tagine, covered, in moderately slow oven 1 hour. (Can be made ahead to this stage. Cover; refrigerate overnight.)

5 Meanwhile, make tunisian-style rice.

6 Remove tagine from oven. Stir in lemon, olives and fresh coriander just before serving; serve with rice.

TUNISIAN-STYLE RICE Wash rice in strainer under cold water until water runs clear; drain. Melt butter in large saucepan, add rice; stir until rice is coated in butter. Add the water; bring to a boil. Reduce heat; simmer rice, partially covered, about 10 minutes or until steam holes appear on the surface. Cover rice tightly, reduce heat to as low as possible; steam 10 minutes (do not remove lid). Remove from heat; stand 10 minutes without removing lid. Fluff with fork before serving.

serves 8
per serving 35.5g fat; 3377kJ (807 cal)

beef bourguignon

PREPARATION TIME 30 MINUTES **COOKING TIME** 2 HOURS 30 MINUTES

A French classic, this dish was favoured dinner-party fare 20 or 30 years ago… and, thanks to the resurgence in popularity of rich and rustic comfort food, it has now reappeared on restaurant menus and in the repertoire of the keen home cook. Shallots, also called french shallots, golden shallots or eschalots, are small, elongated members of the onion family that grow in tight clusters similarly to garlic.

350g shallots

2 tablespoons olive oil

2kg gravy beef, trimmed, chopped coarsely

30g butter

4 bacon rashers (280g), rind removed, chopped coarsely

400g mushrooms, halved

2 cloves garlic, crushed

¼ cup (35g) plain flour

1¼ cups (310ml) beef stock

2½ cups (625ml) dry red wine

2 bay leaves

2 sprigs fresh thyme

½ cup coarsely chopped fresh flat-leaf parsley

1 Peel shallots, leaving root end intact so shallot remains whole during cooking.

2 Heat oil in large flameproof casserole dish; cook beef, in batches, until browned.

3 Heat butter in same dish; cook shallots, bacon, mushrooms and garlic, stirring, until shallots are browned lightly.

4 Sprinkle flour over shallot mixture; cook, stirring, until flour mixture thickens and bubbles. Gradually add stock and wine; stir over heat until mixture boils and thickens. Return beef and any juices to dish, add bay leaves and thyme; bring to a boil. Reduce heat; simmer, covered, about 2 hours or until beef is tender, stirring every 30 minutes. (Can be made ahead to this stage. Cover; refrigerate overnight.)

5 Stir in parsley; discard bay leaves just before serving.

serves 6
per serving 38.3g fat; 2774kJ (663 cal)

braised spatchcock with peas and lettuce

PREPARATION TIME 30 MINUTES **COOKING TIME** 1 HOUR

3 x 500g spatchcocks
1 medium leek (350g)
2 bay leaves
1 sprig fresh thyme
1 sprig fresh rosemary
4 fresh flat-leaf parsley stalks
50g butter
2 cloves garlic, crushed
1 large brown onion (200g),
    chopped finely
8 bacon rashers (560g), rinds
    removed, chopped coarsely
¼ cup (35g) plain flour
1½ cups (375ml) dry white wine
3 cups (750ml) chicken stock
1.5kg potatoes, chopped coarsely
¾ cup (180ml) milk
50g butter
500g frozen peas
1 large butter lettuce,
    shredded finely
½ cup coarsely chopped
    fresh mint

1 Cut along both sides of spatchcocks' backbones; discard backbones. Cut in half between breasts. Rinse spatchcock halves under cold water; pat dry.

2 Cut leek in half crossways; chop white bottom half finely, reserve. Using kitchen string, tie green top half of leek, bay leaves, thyme, rosemary and parsley stalks into a bundle.

3 Heat butter in large saucepan; cook spatchcock, in batches, until browned lightly both sides. Cook reserved chopped leek, garlic, onion and bacon in same pan, stirring, about 10 minutes or until onion softens. Add flour; cook, stirring, 2 minutes. Gradually add wine and stock; bring to a boil, stirring constantly until mixture boils and thickens. Return spatchcock to pan with herb bundle, reduce heat; simmer, covered, 30 minutes. (Can be made ahead to this stage. Cover; refrigerate overnight.)

4 Meanwhile, boil, steam or microwave potato until tender; drain. Mash potato with warmed milk and butter in large bowl until smooth. Cover to keep warm.

5 Discard herb bundle. Add peas, lettuce and mint to pan; simmer, uncovered, about 5 minutes or until peas are just tender. Divide mashed potato among serving plates; top with spatchcock mixture.

serves 6
per serving 42.5g fat; 3294kJ (787 cal)
tip Chicken pieces, quails or pigeons can be used rather than spatchcocks, if desired.

Use scissors to cut away the backbone of each spatchcock.

Cut leek in half crossways; chop the white bottom half finely.

Using kitchen string, tie green top half of leek with herbs into bundle.

octopus braised in red wine

PREPARATION TIME 15 MINUTES **COOKING TIME** 1 HOUR 45 MINUTES

Ask your fishmonger to clean the octopus and remove the beaks.

⅓ cup (80ml) olive oil

600g baby onions, halved

4 cloves garlic, crushed

1.5kg cleaned baby
   octopus, halved

1½ cups (375ml) dry red wine

⅓ cup (95g) tomato paste

⅓ cup (80ml) red wine vinegar

3 large tomatoes (660g), peeled,
   seeded, chopped coarsely

2 bay leaves

1 fresh long red chilli,
   chopped finely

10 drained anchovy fillets (30g),
   chopped coarsely

⅓ cup finely chopped
   fresh oregano

1 cup coarsely chopped fresh
   flat-leaf parsley

1 Heat oil in large saucepan; cook onion and garlic, stirring, until onion softens. Add octopus; cook, stirring, until just changed in colour.

2 Add wine; cook, stirring, about 5 minutes or until pan liquid is reduced by about a third. Add tomato paste, vinegar, tomato, bay leaves, chilli and anchovies; bring to a boil. Reduce heat; simmer, covered, 1 hour. Uncover; simmer about 30 minutes or until sauce thickens and octopus is tender.

3 Stir in oregano and parsley off the heat; serve with thick slices of toasted Italian ciabatta, if desired.

serves 6

per serving 17.5g fat; 2145kJ (512 cal)

panang pork curry with pickled snake beans

PREPARATION TIME 30 MINUTES (PLUS COOLING AND REFRIGERATION TIMES)
COOKING TIME 1 HOUR 30 MINUTES

This curry is a good introduction to the taste of Thai food; while not too chilli-hot, it is full of the individual flavours that have given this cuisine so many devotees. Keep the roots from the coriander as they are used – cleaned and chopped – in the paste. This recipe makes 1 cup of panang curry paste which will keep, tightly covered, in the refrigerator for up to a week.

2¾ cups (680ml) coconut milk
3⅓ cups (830ml) water
1.5kg pork shoulder, trimmed,
    cut into 2cm cubes
1⅔ cups (410ml) coconut cream
¼ cup (65g) grated palm sugar
¼ cup (60ml) fish sauce
6 kaffir lime leaves, sliced thinly
190g can sliced bamboo
    shoots, drained
⅓ cup coarsely chopped
    fresh thai basil
¼ cup coarsely chopped
    fresh coriander
2 fresh long red chillies, seeded,
    sliced thinly

PICKLED SNAKE BEANS
350g snake beans, trimmed
1 cup (250ml) water
1 cup (250ml) white vinegar
1 tablespoon malt vinegar
1 cup (220g) sugar
2 tablespoons salt

PANANG PASTE
6 fresh long red chillies,
    chopped coarsely
2 teaspoons coarsely chopped
    coriander root
2 tablespoons finely chopped
    fresh galangal
10cm stick fresh lemon grass
    (20g), chopped finely
2 thai purple shallots,
    chopped coarsely
3 cloves garlic, peeled, quartered
¼ cup (60ml) water
½ cup (75g) roasted
    unsalted peanuts

1 Make pickled snake beans. (Can be made a day ahead, cover; refrigerate overnight.)

2 Make panang paste. Measure ⅓ cup of the paste for this recipe, then freeze the remainder, covered, for future use. (Can be made a day ahead, cover; refrigerate overnight.)

3 Combine half of the coconut milk and the water in medium saucepan; bring to a boil. Add pork; bring to a boil. Reduce heat; simmer, uncovered, about 1 hour or until tender. Remove pan from heat; cool pork in liquid 30 minutes.

4 Heat coconut cream in large saucepan over heat for about 10 minutes or until fat separates from cream. Add the ⅓ cup panang paste; cook, stirring, 10 minutes. Stir palm sugar and fish sauce into mixture; after sugar dissolves, add 1 cup pork cooking liquid (discard any that remains). Stir in remaining coconut milk, lime leaves, bamboo shoots and drained pork; simmer, uncovered, until heated through.

5 Stir basil and coriander through curry off the heat just before serving, sprinkle with chilli; serve with pickled snake beans and, if desired, steamed jasmine rice.

PICKLED SNAKE BEANS Cut beans into 5cm lengths; place in medium heatproof bowl. Combine the water, vinegars, sugar and salt in small saucepan; stir over heat until sugar dissolves. Bring to a boil, then immediately remove from heat; cool pickling liquid 10 minutes, then pour over beans. Refrigerate beans, covered, 3 hours or overnight before serving.
PANANG PASTE Blend or process chilli, coriander root, galangal, lemon grass, shallot, garlic and the water until mixture forms a smooth paste; add peanuts, pulse until just combined.

serves 6
per serving 42.5g fat; 3258kJ (778 cal)

onion and fennel risotto with chicken meatballs

PREPARATION TIME 40 MINUTES **COOKING TIME** 3 HOURS 30 MINUTES

Chicken shops generally sell raw carcasses in 1kg packages but, if not available, ask the shop for a kilo of mixed chicken backs, necks and bones removed from breast and thigh fillets.

3 litres (12 cups) water

1kg chicken bones

1 large carrot (180g), chopped coarsely

1 trimmed celery stalk (100g), chopped coarsely

1 small brown onion (80g), chopped coarsely

1 bay leaf

2 sprigs fresh flat-leaf parsley

1 teaspoon black peppercorns

2 cups (500ml) dry white wine

1 tablespoon olive oil

20g butter

2 medium brown onions (300g), sliced thinly

1 large fennel (550g), trimmed, sliced thinly

3 cups (600g) arborio rice

2 cloves garlic, crushed

1 cup (80g) coarsely grated parmesan cheese

2 tablespoons finely chopped fresh tarragon

CHICKEN MEATBALLS

2 tablespoons olive oil

1 medium leek (350g), sliced thinly

500g chicken mince

1 egg

1 clove garlic, crushed

¾ cup (50g) stale breadcrumbs

1 tablespoon finely chopped fresh tarragon

1 Combine the water, chicken bones, carrot, celery, chopped onion, bay leaf, parsley and peppercorns in large saucepan; bring to a boil. Reduce heat; simmer, uncovered, 2½ hours. Strain stock through muslin-lined sieve or colander into large bowl; discard solids. (Can be made ahead to this stage. Cover; refrigerate overnight.) Return stock to same cleaned pan with wine; bring to a boil. Reduce heat; simmer, covered.

2 Heat oil and butter in large saucepan; cook sliced onion and fennel, stirring, over low heat about 15 minutes or until vegetables soften and are browned lightly.

3 Meanwhile, make chicken meatballs.

4 Add rice and garlic to pan with vegetables; stir to coat in butter mixture. Stir in 1 cup of the simmering stock mixture; cook, stirring, over low heat until liquid is absorbed. Continue adding stock mixture, in 1-cup batches, stirring, until liquid is absorbed after each addition. Total cooking time should be about 35 minutes or until rice is just tender. Gently stir chicken meatballs, cheese and half of the tarragon into risotto; serve sprinkled with remaining tarragon.

CHICKEN MEATBALLS Heat half of the oil in large frying pan; cook leek, stirring, about 5 minutes or until softened. Place leek with remaining ingredients in medium bowl; using hands, mix until combined. Roll level tablespoons of the mixture into balls. Heat remaining oil in same frying pan; cook meatballs, shaking pan occasionally, until browned all over and cooked through.

serves 6

per serving 24.8g fat; 3195kJ (763 cal)

vegetable tagine with harissa and almond couscous

PREPARATION TIME 30 MINUTES **COOKING TIME** 30 MINUTES

Harissa, a North African paste made from dried red chillies, garlic, olive oil and caraway seeds, can be used as a rub for meat, an ingredient in sauces and dressings, or eaten on its own, as a condiment. It is available ready-made from all Middle-Eastern food shops and some supermarkets.

20g butter

1 tablespoon olive oil

2 medium brown onions (300g),
    chopped coarsely

2 cloves garlic, crushed

4cm piece fresh ginger
    (20g), grated

2 teaspoons ground cumin

2 teaspoons ground coriander

2 teaspoons finely grated
    lemon rind

1kg pumpkin, chopped coarsely

400g can chopped tomatoes

2 cups (500ml) vegetable stock

400g green beans, cut into
    5cm lengths

⅓ cup (55g) sultanas

1 tablespoon honey

¼ cup finely chopped fresh
    flat-leaf parsley

¼ cup finely chopped fresh mint

HARISSA AND
ALMOND COUSCOUS

2 cups (500ml) vegetable stock

1 cup (250ml) water

3 cups (600g) couscous

½ cup (70g) toasted
    slivered almonds

1 tablespoon harissa

1   Heat butter and oil in large saucepan; cook onion and garlic, stirring, 5 minutes. Add ginger, spices and rind; cook about 1 minute or until fragrant. Add pumpkin, undrained tomatoes and stock; bring to a boil. Reduce heat; simmer, covered, about 15 minutes or until pumpkin is just tender.

2   Meanwhile, make harissa and almond couscous.

3   Stir beans into tagine mixture; cook, stirring, 5 minutes. Stir sultanas, honey and chopped herbs through tagine off the heat just before serving; serve with couscous.

HARISSA AND ALMOND COUSCOUS Bring stock and the water to a boil in medium saucepan; remove from heat. Add couscous; cover, stand about 3 minutes or until liquid is absorbed, fluffing with fork occasionally. Use fork to gently mix almonds and harissa through couscous.

serves 6
per serving 14.4g fat; 2668kJ (637 cal)

beef and horseradish stew with kumara potato mash

PREPARATION TIME 40 MINUTES **COOKING TIME** 3 HOURS 30 MINUTES

2 tablespoons olive oil

1.5kg beef chuck steak, cut into 5cm cubes

3 medium brown onions (450g), sliced into wedges

3 cloves garlic, crushed

8cm piece fresh ginger (40g), grated

2 teaspoons curry powder

¼ cup (35g) plain flour

3 cups (750ml) beef stock

1 tablespoon worcestershire sauce

2 tablespoons horseradish cream

¼ cup coarsely chopped fresh flat-leaf parsley

KUMARA POTATO MASH

1kg kumara, chopped coarsely

500g potatoes, chopped coarsely

¾ cup (180ml) cream

50g butter

1 Preheat oven to very slow.

2 Heat oil in large flameproof casserole dish; cook beef, in batches, until browned. Cook onion, garlic and ginger in same dish, stirring, about 5 minutes or until onion softens. Add curry powder and flour; cook, stirring, 5 minutes.

3 Return beef to dish with stock and worcestershire sauce; stir over heat until mixture boils and thickens. Cover dish tightly; cook in very slow oven for 3 hours, stirring occasionally. (Can be made ahead to this stage. Cover; refrigerate overnight or freeze.)

4 Meanwhile, make kumara potato mash.

5 Stir horseradish cream and parsley through beef mixture off the heat just before serving; serve with kumara potato mash.

KUMARA POTATO MASH Boil, steam or microwave kumara and potato, separately, until tender; drain. Mash kumara and potato with warmed cream and butter in large bowl until smooth; cover to keep warm.

serves 6
per serving 40.4g fat; 3150kJ (752 cal)

osso buco

PREPARATION TIME 45 MINUTES **COOKING TIME** 2 HOURS 35 MINUTES

Ask your butcher to cut the veal shin into fairly thick (about 4cm) pieces for you.

12 pieces veal osso buco (2.5kg)
¼ cup (35g) plain flour
¼ cup (60ml) olive oil
40g butter
1 medium brown onion (150g),
    chopped coarsely
2 cloves garlic, crushed
3 trimmed celery stalks (300g),
    chopped coarsely
2 large carrots (360g),
    chopped coarsely
4 medium tomatoes (600g),
    chopped coarsely
2 tablespoons tomato paste
1 cup (250ml) dry white wine
1 cup (250ml) beef stock
400g can crushed tomatoes
3 sprigs fresh thyme
¼ cup coarsely chopped fresh
    flat-leaf parsley

GREMOLATA
1 tablespoon finely grated
    lemon rind
⅓ cup finely chopped fresh
    flat-leaf parsley
2 cloves garlic, chopped finely

1 Toss veal and flour together, in batches, in paper or plastic bag; remove veal from bag, shake away excess flour.
2 Heat oil in large flameproof casserole dish; cook veal, in batches, until browned all over.
3 Melt butter in same dish; cook onion, garlic, celery and carrot, stirring, until vegetables soften. Stir in tomato, tomato paste, wine, stock, undrained crushed tomatoes and herbs.
4 Return veal to dish, fitting pieces upright and tightly together in a single layer; bring to a boil. Cover, reduce heat; simmer 1¾ hours. Uncover; cook 30 minutes. (Can be made ahead to this stage. Cover; refrigerate overnight.)
5 Meanwhile, make gremolata.
6 Remove veal from dish; cover to keep warm. Bring sauce to a boil; boil, uncovered, about 10 minutes or until sauce thickens slightly.
7 Divide veal among serving plates; top with sauce, sprinkle with gremolata. Serve with mashed potato or soft polenta, if desired.

GREMOLATA Combine ingredients in small bowl. Cover with plastic wrap and refrigerate until required.

serves 6
per serving 18.9g fat; 2100kJ (502 cal)

Toss veal and flour together, in batches, in paper or plastic bag.

The casserole dish should only be big enough to fit all the pieces of meat snugly in a single layer.

The garlic, rind and parsley should be chopped to exactly the same size for the gremolata.

asian-spiced roasted pork belly

PREPARATION TIME 10 MINUTES (PLUS REFRIGERATION TIME) **COOKING TIME** 1 HOUR 25 MINUTES

1kg pork belly, skin on, boned
½ cup (125ml) chinese
    cooking wine
¼ cup (60ml) soy sauce
1 tablespoon tamarind
    concentrate
2 tablespoons honey
½ teaspoon sesame oil
4cm piece fresh ginger (20g),
    chopped finely
3 cloves garlic, crushed
2 teaspoons five-spice powder
1 star anise
1 dried long red chilli
1 teaspoon sichuan pepper
3 cups (750ml) water
900g baby bok choy,
    halved lengthways

1 Place pork in large saucepan of boiling water; return
  to a boil. Reduce heat; simmer, uncovered, about
  40 minutes or until pork is cooked through, drain.

2 Meanwhile, combine wine, soy, tamarind, honey, oil,
  ginger, garlic, five-spice, star anise, chilli, pepper and
  the water in large bowl. Add pork; turn to coat pork in
  marinade. Cover; refrigerate 3 hours or overnight.

3 Preheat oven to hot.

4 Place pork, skin-side up, on wire rack in large
  shallow baking dish; reserve marinade. Pour enough
  water into baking dish to come halfway up side of
  dish. Roast pork, uncovered, in hot oven about
  30 minutes or until browned.

5 Meanwhile, strain marinade into small saucepan;
  bring to a boil. Boil, uncovered, about 20 minutes
  or until sauce reduces to about 1 cup. Boil, steam
  or microwave bok choy until just tender; drain.

6 Serve pork with sauce and bok choy and, if desired,
  steamed jasmine rice.

serves 6
per serving 34.2g fat; 2035kJ (486 cal)

raan with lemon pilau

PREPARATION TIME 25 MINUTES (PLUS REFRIGERATION TIME) **COOKING TIME** 2 HOURS 35 MINUTES

When you're invited home for a lamb roast in northern India, this traditional recipe is probably what you'll be served. Try cooking it for your next Sunday dinner with your family and we bet they'll cancel any other plans.

2 teaspoons coriander seeds

1 teaspoon cumin seeds

5 cardamom pods, bruised

1 teaspoon chilli powder

1 teaspoon ground turmeric

1 cinnamon stick

2 cloves

2 star anise

1 medium brown onion (150g),
   chopped coarsely

4 cloves garlic, peeled

2cm piece fresh ginger (10g),
   grated finely

¼ cup (40g) blanched almonds

½ cup (140g) yogurt

2 tablespoons lemon juice

2kg leg of lamb, trimmed

LEMON PILAU

1 tablespoon vegetable oil

5 cardamom pods, bruised

4 cloves

1 cinnamon stick

¼ teaspoon saffron threads

2 cups (400g) white long-grain rice

3 cups (750ml) boiling water

⅓ cup (80ml) lemon juice

1 tablespoon sugar

20g butter

2 teaspoons finely grated
   lemon rind

2 tablespoons slivered
   toasted almonds

1 Dry-fry seeds, cardamom, chilli, turmeric, cinnamon, cloves and star anise in heated small frying pan, stirring, about 2 minutes or until fragrant. Blend or process spices with onion, garlic, ginger, nuts, yogurt and juice until mixture forms a paste.

2 Pierce lamb all over with sharp knife; place on wire rack in large shallow baking dish. Spread paste over lamb, pressing firmly into cuts. Cover; refrigerate overnight. (Can be made up to 2 days ahead to this stage. Cover; refrigerate, or freeze if desired.)

3 Preheat oven to moderately hot. Remove lamb from refrigerator; pour enough water into baking dish to completely cover base. Cover dish with foil; roast lamb in moderately hot oven 30 minutes. Reduce oven temperature to slow; roast lamb, covered with foil, 1½ hours. Uncover; roast about 30 minutes or until lamb is cooked as desired.

4 Meanwhile, make lemon pilau.

5 Cover lamb; stand 10 minutes before slicing. Serve with pilau and, if desired, yogurt with coarsely chopped fresh coriander stirred through it.

LEMON PILAU Heat oil in large saucepan; cook spices, stirring, about 1 minute or until fragrant. Add rice; stir until rice is coated in spice mixture. Add the water, juice and sugar; bring to a boil. Reduce heat; simmer rice, partially covered, about 10 minutes or until steam holes appear on surface. Reduce heat to as low as possible, cover rice tightly; steam 10 minutes (do not remove lid). Remove from heat; stand 10 minutes without removing lid. Fluff with fork, then stir in butter, rind and nuts before serving.

serves 6

per serving 25.9g fat; 3012kJ (719 cal)

duck with pistachio stuffing and warm kipfler salad

PREPARATION TIME 1 HOUR 10 MINUTES (PLUS STANDING TIME) **COOKING TIME** 1 HOUR

200g pork mince

200g chicken mince

150g chicken livers, trimmed, chopped finely

1 cup (70g) stale breadcrumbs

2 tablespoons coarsely chopped fresh sage

¼ cup finely chopped fresh flat-leaf parsley

½ cup (75g) shelled pistachios

1 teaspoon juniper berries, chopped coarsely

1 teaspoon five-spice powder

2 eggs, beaten lightly

900g boned duck

2 teaspoons olive oil

2 teaspoons sea salt flakes

500g baby green beans

WARM KIPFLER SALAD

1.5kg kipfler potatoes

¼ cup (60ml) olive oil

1 medium brown onion (150g), chopped finely

2 bacon rashers (140g), rind removed, chopped finely

½ cup (125ml) dry white wine

1½ cups (375ml) chicken stock

¼ cup finely chopped fresh flat-leaf parsley

1 Using hand, combine both minces, liver, breadcrumbs, herbs, nuts, berries, five-spice and eggs in medium bowl.

2 Place duck, skin-side down, on board; using hand, mound stuffing lengthways along centre of duck. Fold one long side of duck over mixture, then overlap with the other. Skewer duck at intervals to hold securely together; tie kitchen string around duck between each skewer to secure tightly. Place duck in lightly oiled large baking dish; rub all over with oil then salt. Roast, uncovered, in moderate oven about 1 hour or until duck is cooked as desired. Cover; stand 15 minutes before slicing. Discard skewers and string.

3 Meanwhile, make warm kipfler salad.

4 Boil, steam or microwave beans until tender; drain.

5 Divide beans and salad among serving plates; top with slices of duck.

WARM KIPFLER SALAD Boil, steam or microwave unpeeled potatoes until almost tender; drain. Rinse under cold water; drain, peel. Combine potatoes and 2 tablespoons of the oil in large bowl; place potatoes, in single layer, on oven tray. Roast, uncovered, in moderate oven about 20 minutes or until potatoes are browned lightly. Meanwhile, heat remaining oil in medium frying pan; cook onion and bacon, stirring, until onion softens. Add wine; cook until liquid reduces by half. Stir in stock; bring to a boil. Reduce heat; simmer, uncovered, 2 minutes. Place potatoes in large bowl with bacon mixture and parsley; toss gently to combine.

serves 6

per serving 82.6g fat; 4829kJ (1154 cal)

tips Pre-order a boned duck from your local poultry shop or from the poultry section in your supermarket. A 2kg duck, once boned, will weigh approximately 900g and is the correct size for this recipe.

You need eight 10cm bamboo skewers for this recipe.

Place duck skin-side down, then mound stuffing down the centre.

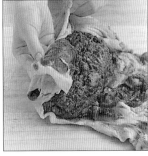
Fold one side of the duck over stuffing, then overlap with the other.

Secure duck closed with skewers, then tie tightly with kitchen string.

snapper, fennel and semi-dried tomato parcels

PREPARATION TIME 35 MINUTES (PLUS FREEZING TIME) **COOKING TIME** 20 MINUTES

A modern take on the traditional French method of cooking "en papillote" (in sealed paper packets), this recipe uses aluminium foil rather than parchment to enclose the ingredients. Cooking this way intensifies the contained flavours.

20g butter
3 baby fennel bulbs (390g),
    trimmed, sliced thinly
¼ cup (60ml) water
⅔ cup (100g) semi-dried tomatoes
2 tablespoons fresh
    oregano leaves
3 cloves garlic, crushed
2 teaspoons finely grated
    lemon rind
2 tablespoons lemon juice
1 tablespoon olive oil
6 x 400g snappers, cleaned

HERB BUTTER
60g butter, softened
2 tablespoons finely chopped
    fresh oregano
2 tablespoons finely chopped
    fresh flat-leaf parsley

1 Preheat oven to hot. Make herb butter.
2 Melt butter in medium frying pan; cook fennel, stirring, until softened. Remove from heat; blend or process with the water, tomatoes, oregano, garlic, rind, juice and oil until mixture forms a paste.
3 Score each fish three times on both sides; place each fish on a square of lightly oiled foil large enough to completely enclose fish. Top each fish with a sixth of the fennel mixture; gather corners of foil squares together above fish, twist to enclose securely. Place parcels on oven tray; cook in hot oven about 15 minutes or until cooked as desired.
4 Discard foil just before serving; top fish with a slice of the herb butter.

HERB BUTTER Beat ingredients in small bowl until combined. Place on piece of plastic wrap; shape into a log, wrap butter mixture tightly in plastic wrap. Place in refrigerator until firm; remove 15 minutes before serving.

serves 6
per serving 17.8g fat; 1360kJ (325 cal)

eggplant pastitsio

PREPARATION TIME 40 MINUTES **COOKING TIME** 1 HOUR 20 MINUTES

Pastitsio is to Greeks as lasagne is to Italians – a layered meat and pasta bake
traditionally made with a rich herbed tomato mixture and creamy white sauce.
Bavette is a long, flat pasta similar to linguine and is sold at most supermarkets.

2 large eggplants (1kg)

150g bavette

30g butter, melted

3 eggs, beaten lightly

⅓ cup (25g) finely grated
    parmesan cheese

¼ cup finely chopped fresh basil

¼ cup finely chopped fresh
    flat-leaf parsley

½ teaspoon ground nutmeg

500g lamb mince

1 teaspoon olive oil

1 medium brown onion (150g),
    chopped finely

1 clove garlic, crushed

½ teaspoon ground cinnamon

1 tablespoon tomato paste

¼ cup (60ml) dry red wine

¼ cup (60ml) beef stock

425g can crushed tomatoes

WHITE SAUCE

60g butter

⅓ cup (50g) plain flour

2 cups (500ml) milk

1 Preheat oven to hot. Cut eggplants lengthways into very thin slices;
place eggplant, in single layer, on oiled oven trays, cover with foil. Bake
in hot oven about 25 minutes or until eggplant is softened and browned.
Remove eggplant from oven.

2 Reduce oven temperature to moderate.

3 Meanwhile, cook pasta in medium saucepan of boiling water, uncovered,
until just tender; drain. Rinse under cold water; drain. Combine in medium
bowl with butter, eggs, cheese, herbs and nutmeg.

4 Cook lamb in heated large non-stick frying pan, stirring, until changed
in colour; remove lamb, then drain pan. Heat oil in same pan; cook
onion and garlic, stirring, about 2 minutes or until onion softens. Return
lamb to pan with cinnamon and tomato paste; cook, stirring, 2 minutes.
Add wine, stock and undrained tomatoes; bring to a boil. Reduce heat;
simmer, uncovered, stirring occasionally, about 15 minutes or until sauce
thickens. (Can be made ahead to this stage. Cover; refrigerate overnight.)

5 Meanwhile, make white sauce.

6 Grease deep 22cm round cake pan; line base and side with two-thirds
of the eggplant. Place half of the pasta mixture in pan; cover with white
sauce. Spread lamb sauce over white sauce; top with remaining pasta
mixture. Use remaining eggplant to completely cover pastitsio; cover
tightly with foil. Cook in moderate oven about 30 minutes or until heated
through. Stand 10 minutes before serving.

WHITE SAUCE Melt butter in medium saucepan, add flour; cook, stirring,
about 2 minutes or until mixture thickens and bubbles. Gradually stir in
milk; cook, stirring, until sauce boils and thickens.

serves 8
per serving 22g fat; 1664kJ (398 cal)
tip Bucatini or macaroni can be used if bavette is unavailable.

On a lightly floured surface, roll dough into a 2cm-thick sausage.

Cut sausage shapes into 2cm pieces then roll pieces into balls.

Roll ball over inside of fork, press ball's centre to form classic shape.

vegetable gnocchi with cheese sauce

PREPARATION TIME 2 HOURS (PLUS REFRIGERATION TIME) **COOKING TIME** 40 MINUTES

Gnocchi should be light, delicate, pillow-like dumplings which virtually melt in the mouth. The russet burbank potato is ideal for making gnocchi because its low water content means less flour is needed to make the dough stick together – the result is a lighter dumpling. Idaho, bintje and spunta potatoes are also acceptable for making gnocchi.

1.2kg russet burbank potatoes
1 medium (400g) kumara
300g spinach, trimmed, chopped coarsely
3 eggs
½ cup (40g) coarsely grated parmesan cheese
2 cups (300g) plain flour
2 tablespoons olive oil
100g blue cheese, crumbled
⅓ cup (25g) finely grated pecorino cheese

CHEESE SAUCE
30g butter
2 tablespoons plain flour
2½ cups (625ml) milk
⅔ cup (160ml) cream
½ cup (50g) finely grated gruyère cheese
⅔ cup (50g) finely grated pecorino cheese

1 Boil or steam unpeeled potatoes until tender; drain. Peel when cool enough to handle; chop coarsely.

2 Meanwhile, microwave unpeeled kumara on HIGH (100%) about 8 minutes or until tender; drain. Peel when cool enough to handle. Boil, steam or microwave spinach until wilted; drain.

3 Using wooden spoon, push potato through fine sieve or mouli into large bowl. Divide potato mash among three medium bowls; stir one egg into each bowl until mixture is combined. Using wooden spoon, push kumara through fine sieve into one of the bowls; stir to combine. Stir parmesan cheese into the second bowl and spinach into the third; stir to combine. Add approximately ⅓ cup of flour to each bowl; stir each potato mixture to make a firm dough.

4 Roll each portion of dough on lightly floured surface into 2cm-thick sausage shape. Cut each sausage shape into 2cm pieces; roll pieces into balls. Roll each ball along the inside tines of a fork, pressing lightly on top of ball with index finger to form classic gnocchi shape – grooves on one side and a dimple on the other. Place gnocchi, in single layer, on lightly floured trays, cover; refrigerate 1 hour.

5 Cook gnocchi, in batches, uncovered, in large saucepan of boiling water about 2 minutes or until gnocchi float to surface. Remove from pan with slotted spoon; drain. Gently toss gnocchi in large bowl with oil.

6 Make cheese sauce. Pour sauce over gnocchi; toss gently to coat. Divide gnocchi among six lightly oiled 1½-cup (375ml) ovenproof dishes; sprinkle with blue then pecorino cheeses. Place under hot grill about 3 minutes or until cheese browns lightly.

CHEESE SAUCE Melt butter in medium saucepan. Add flour; cook, stirring, until mixture thickens and bubbles. Gradually add milk and cream; stir until mixture boils and thickens. Remove from heat; stir in cheeses.

serves 6
per serving 40.9g fat; 3313kJ (791 cal)
tip It's a good idea to cook the kumara in the microwave oven to keep water absorption to the barest minimum.

veal rack with roast pumpkin risotto

PREPARATION TIME 30 MINUTES (PLUS REFRIGERATION TIME) **COOKING TIME** 5 HOURS 30 MINUTES

Risotto, a creamy rice dish originally from northern Italy, is now so wildly popular, it's almost impossible to find a café or restaurant menu that doesn't list one of its seemingly infinite variations.

1kg veal shin, cut into pieces
1 medium brown onion (150g),
    chopped coarsely
1 trimmed celery stalk (100g),
    chopped coarsely
1 medium carrot (120g),
    chopped coarsely
2 bay leaves
1 teaspoon black peppercorns
4 litres (16 cups) water
2 cloves garlic, crushed
2 tablespoons finely chopped
    fresh rosemary
2 tablespoons wholegrain mustard
1 tablespoon olive oil
1.2kg veal rack (6-cutlet)

ROAST PUMPKIN RISOTTO
500g pumpkin, chopped coarsely
2 tablespoons olive oil
1 medium brown onion (150g),
    chopped finely
1½ cups (300g) arborio rice
½ cup (125ml) dry white wine
¼ cup (20g) finely grated
    parmesan cheese
20g butter
⅓ cup finely chopped fresh
    flat-leaf parsley

1 Preheat oven to hot. Place veal shin and onion in baking dish; roast, uncovered, in hot oven about 1 hour or until bones are well browned. Transfer bones and onions to large saucepan with celery, carrot, bay leaves, peppercorns and the water; bring to a boil. Reduce heat; simmer, uncovered, 3 hours. Strain stock through muslin-lined sieve or colander into large bowl; discard solids. Allow stock to cool, cover; refrigerate until cold. (Can be made ahead to this stage. Cover; refrigerate overnight.)

2 Reduce oven temperature to moderate.

3 Combine garlic, rosemary, mustard and oil in small bowl. Place veal on wire rack over large shallow baking dish; spread garlic mixture over veal rack. Roast, covered, in moderate oven 1 hour. Uncover; roast in moderate oven 30 minutes or until cooked as desired. Cover; stand 10 minutes.

4 Meanwhile, make roast pumpkin risotto.

5 Serve veal, sliced into cutlets, with risotto.

ROAST PUMPKIN RISOTTO About 45 minutes into veal roasting time, place pumpkin on oven tray; drizzle with half of the oil. Roast, uncovered, in moderate oven with veal about 45 minutes or until browned and tender. Meanwhile, skim fat from surface of stock; place stock in large saucepan, bring to a boil. Reduce heat; simmer, covered. Heat remaining oil in large saucepan; cook onion, stirring, until soft. Add rice; stir to coat in onion mixture. Stir in wine; cook, stirring, until liquid is absorbed. Add ½ cup of the simmering stock; cook, stirring, over low heat until stock is absorbed. Continue adding stock, in ½-cup batches, stirring, until stock is absorbed after each addition. Total cooking time should be about 35 minutes or until rice is tender. Just before serving, stir roast pumpkin, cheese, butter and parsley into risotto.

serves 6
per serving 15.4g fat; 2135kJ (510 cal)

barbecue spare ribs

PREPARATION TIME 25 MINUTES (PLUS REFRIGERATION TIME) **COOKING TIME** 2 HOURS 10 MINUTES

Ask your butcher to cut pork spare ribs "American-style" for this recipe. Trimmed of almost all fat, the meat usually comes in slabs of 8 to 10 ribs.

3.5kg slabs of american-style
   pork spare ribs

BARBECUE SAUCE
2¼ cups (560ml) tomato sauce
1½ cups (375ml) apple
   cider vinegar
⅓ cup (80ml) olive oil
½ cup (125ml) worcestershire
   sauce
¾ cup (165g) firmly packed
   brown sugar
⅓ cup (95g) american-style
   mustard
1½ teaspoons cracked
   black pepper
3 fresh red thai chillies,
   chopped finely
3 cloves garlic, crushed
¼ cup (60ml) lemon juice

1 Make barbecue sauce.
2 Place slabs of ribs in large deep baking dish; brush both sides of each slab with sauce. Pour remaining sauce over slabs, cover; refrigerate overnight, turning slabs occasionally in the sauce.
3 Preheat oven to moderately slow. Drain slabs, reserving sauce. Divide slabs of ribs between two wire racks over two large shallow baking dishes. Roast, covered, in moderately slow oven 1½ hours, uncovering to brush with sauce every 20 minutes. Turn slabs midway through cooking time.
4 Increase oven temperature to hot. Uncover slabs; bake in hot oven, brushing frequently with sauce, until slabs are browned and cooked through, turning after 15 minutes.
5 Place remaining barbecue sauce in small saucepan; bring to a boil. Reduce heat; simmer, stirring, about 4 minutes or until sauce thickens slightly. Using scissors, cut slabs in portions of two or three ribs; serve ribs with hot barbecue sauce.

BARBECUE SAUCE Combine ingredients in medium saucepan; bring to a boil. Remove from heat; cool before brushing over ribs.

serves 8
per serving 25.5g fat; 2404kJ (574 cal)
tip You'll save on cleaning time if you line the bases of the baking dishes with baking paper.
serving suggestion Serve with your favourite potato salad or vinaigrette-dressed coleslaw.

apple-stuffed pork loin with braised red cabbage

PREPARATION TIME 1 HOUR **COOKING TIME** 2 HOURS 15 MINUTES

When you order the pork loin, ask your butcher to leave a flap measuring about 20cm in length to help make rolling the stuffed loin easier. And, since his knives are probably sharper than yours, why not see if he will remove the rind for the crackling!

2.5kg boneless pork loin with
    20cm flap
2 tablespoons coarse cooking salt
3 cups (750ml) sparkling
    apple cider
½ cup (125ml) chicken stock
3 teaspoons sugar

APPLE STUFFING

30g butter
3 large granny smith apples
    (600g), peeled, cored, cut into
    thin wedges
1 medium leek (350g), sliced thinly
1 medium brown onion (150g),
    sliced thinly
½ teaspoon ground cinnamon
2 tablespoons sugar
1 cup (70g) stale breadcrumbs
1 tablespoon finely grated
    lemon rind
1 cup coarsely chopped fresh
    flat-leaf parsley

BRAISED CABBAGE

40g butter
¼ teaspoon caraway seeds
4 sprigs thyme
1 bay leaf
1 medium brown onion (150g),
    chopped finely
1 medium granny smith apple
    (150g), peeled, grated coarsely
1.5kg red cabbage, sliced thinly
½ cup (125ml) red wine vinegar
1¼ cups (310ml) water

1 Preheat oven to very hot.
2 Place pork on board, rind-side up. Run sharp knife about 5mm under rind, gradually lifting rind away from pork. Place rind in large shallow baking dish. Using sharp knife, make shallow cuts in one direction diagonally across fat at 3cm intervals, then shallow-cut in opposite direction, forming diamonds; rub with salt. Roast, uncovered, in very hot oven about 30 minutes or until crackling is browned and crisp. Chop crackling into serving pieces; reserve. Reduce oven temperature to moderate.
3 Meanwhile, make apple stuffing.
4 Slice through the thickest part of pork horizontally, without cutting all the way through. Open pork out to form one large piece; press stuffing against the loin along length of pork. Roll pork to enclose stuffing; secure with kitchen string at 2cm intervals.
5 Place pork on rack in large shallow flameproof baking dish; pour 2½ cups of the cider into dish. Roast, uncovered, in moderate oven about 1½ hours or until cooked through.
6 Meanwhile, make braised cabbage.
7 Remove pork from baking dish; cover to keep warm. Place baking dish over heat, add stock, sugar and remaining cider; cook, stirring, until sauce thickens slightly.
8 Serve pork, braised cabbage and crackling drizzled with sauce.

APPLE STUFFING Heat butter in large frying pan; cook apple, leek, onion, cinnamon and sugar, stirring, until leek and onion soften. Remove from heat; stir in breadcrumbs, rind and parsley.
BRAISED CABBAGE Place butter, caraway seeds, thyme and bay leaf in large heavy-based saucepan; cook, stirring, until fragrant. Add onion and apple; cook, stirring, until onion softens. Add cabbage, vinegar and the water; cook, covered, over low heat, stirring occasionally, 1 hour. Discard thyme and bay leaf.

serves 8
per serving 104.4g fat; 5550kJ (1326 cal)

lasagne bolognese

PREPARATION TIME I HOUR 15 MINUTES **COOKING TIME** 2 HOURS 45 MINUTES (PLUS STANDING TIME)

This is the way lasagne is traditionally made in Bologna – with chicken liver and milk in the sauce. You'll never go back to your old lasagne recipe again after you taste our version. Semolina flour is made from crushed durum wheat hearts, ground to a very fine flour. It is available at most supermarkets and health food stores.

2 teaspoons olive oil

6 slices pancetta (90g), chopped finely

1 large white onion (200g), chopped finely

1 medium carrot (120g), chopped finely

2 trimmed celery stalks (200g), chopped finely

1kg beef mince

150g chicken livers, trimmed, chopped finely

2 cups (500ml) milk

60g butter

2 cups (500ml) beef stock

1 cup (250ml) dry red wine

410g can tomato puree

2 tablespoons tomato paste

¼ cup finely chopped fresh flat-leaf parsley

2 cups (160g) finely grated parmesan cheese

PASTA

1 cup (150g) plain flour

¼ cup (45g) semolina flour

2 eggs

1 tablespoon olive oil

semolina flour, for dusting, extra

WHITE SAUCE

125g butter

¾ cup (110g) plain flour

1.25 litres (5 cups) hot milk

1 Heat oil in large heavy-based pan; cook pancetta, stirring, until crisp. Add onion, carrot and celery; cook, stirring, until vegetables soften. Add beef and liver; cook, stirring, until beef just changes colour. Stir in milk and butter; cook, stirring occasionally, until liquid reduces to about half. Add stock, wine, puree and paste; simmer, uncovered, 1½ hours. Remove from heat; stir in parsley. (Can be made ahead to this stage. Cover; refrigerate overnight.)

2 Meanwhile, make pasta.

3 Preheat oven to moderately hot. Grease deep 26cm x 35cm baking dish.

4 Make white sauce. Spread about ½ cup of the white sauce over base of dish. Layer two pasta sheets, ¼ of the meat sauce, ¼ cup of the cheese and about 1 cup of the remaining white sauce in dish. Repeat layering process, starting with pasta sheets and ending with white sauce; you will have four layers in total. Top lasagne with remaining cheese.

5 Bake lasagne, uncovered, in moderately hot oven about 40 minutes or until top is browned lightly. Stand 15 minutes before cutting.

PASTA Process flours, eggs and oil until mixture forms a ball. Transfer dough to floured surface; knead about 5 minutes or until smooth. Divide dough into quarters; roll each piece through pasta machine set on thickest setting. Fold long sides of dough into the centre, roll through machine. Repeat rolling several times, adjusting setting so pasta sheets become thinner with each roll; dust pasta with extra semolina flour when necessary. Roll to second thinnest setting (1mm thick), making sure pasta is at least 10cm wide. Cut pasta into 35cm lengths. Cook pasta sheets in large saucepan of boiling salted water, in batches, about 1 minute or until pasta rises to surface. Transfer to bowl of iced water; drain, pat dry with absorbent paper towel.

WHITE SAUCE Melt butter in medium saucepan, add flour; stir until mixture forms a smooth paste. Stir in milk gradually; bring to a boil, stirring, until sauce boils and thickens.

serves 8

per serving 53.1g fat; 3657kJ (874 cal)

tip Fresh or dried lasagne sheets can be substituted for the homemade pasta; follow directions on the packet for cooking time.

chocolate banana bread

PREPARATION TIME 15 MINUTES **COOKING TIME** 1 HOUR

You need about two large overripe bananas (460g) for this recipe.

1 cup mashed banana
¾ cup (165g) caster sugar
2 eggs, beaten lightly
¼ cup (60ml) extra light olive oil
¼ cup (60ml) milk
⅔ cup (100g) self-raising flour
⅔ cup (100g) wholemeal
   self-raising flour
¾ cup (90g) coarsely chopped
   toasted walnuts
¼ cup (45g) finely chopped
   dark eating chocolate

WHIPPED NUT BUTTER
100g butter
¼ cup (30g) finely chopped
   toasted walnuts

1 Preheat oven to moderate. Grease 14cm x 21cm loaf pan; line base and long sides with baking paper.

2 Combine banana and sugar in large bowl; stir in eggs, oil and milk. Add remaining ingredients; stir until combined.

3 Spread mixture into prepared pan; bake, uncovered, in moderate oven about 1 hour. Stand bread in pan 5 minutes; turn onto wire rack to cool. Serve bread warm with whipped nut butter.

WHIPPED NUT BUTTER Beat butter in small bowl with electric mixer until light and fluffy; stir in nuts.

serves 12
per serving 20.8g fat; 1416kJ (338 cal)
tip Leftover banana bread can be toasted if desired.

rosemary pumpkin bread

PREPARATION TIME 20 MINUTES **COOKING TIME** 1 HOUR 40 MINUTES

Polenta, also known as cornmeal, is a flour-like cereal made from dried corn
(maize) sold ground in several different textures and available at most supermarkets.

500g pumpkin, diced into
   1cm pieces
1 tablespoon vegetable oil
1 tablespoon finely chopped
   fresh rosemary
1¾ cups (260g) self-raising flour
¾ cup (125g) polenta
½ cup (40g) finely grated
   parmesan cheese
2 eggs
1¼ cups (300g) sour cream
⅓ cup (55g) pepitas

1 Preheat oven to moderately hot. Grease 14cm x 21cm loaf pan; line base
and long sides with baking paper.

2 Place combined pumpkin, oil and half of the rosemary, in single layer, on
oven tray; roast, uncovered, in moderately hot oven about 20 minutes or
until pumpkin is tender. Cool 10 minutes; mash mixture in medium bowl.
(Can be made ahead to this stage. Cover; refrigerate overnight.)

3 Reduce oven temperature to moderate. Stir flour, polenta, cheese and
remaining rosemary into pumpkin mixture. Whisk eggs and sour cream in
medium jug; pour into mixture, stirring until just combined.

4 Spread mixture into prepared pan; top with pepitas, pressing gently into
surface. Cover with a piece of foil folded with a pleat; bake in moderate
oven 1 hour. Remove foil; bake in moderate oven about 20 minutes.
Stand in pan 5 minutes; turn onto wire rack to cool.

serves 8
per serving 24.5g fat; 1747kJ (417 cal)

dinner rolls

PREPARATION TIME 30 MINUTES (PLUS STANDING TIME) **COOKING TIME** 15 MINUTES

Ever wanted to serve those hot dinner rolls you get in restaurants? Well, now you can. As they are made with bakers' flour (sometimes sold as bread flour), which has a higher gluten content than plain flour, these rolls have a particularly crisp crust. Bakers' flour can be found in most supermarkets and health-food stores.

2 cups (500ml) warm water
1 teaspoon sugar
2 teaspoons (7g) dried yeast
4 cups (640g) bakers' flour
2 teaspoons salt
cooking-oil spray

1 Whisk the water, sugar and yeast in medium jug until yeast dissolves, cover; stand in warm place about 15 minutes or until mixture is frothy.

2 Combine flour and salt in large bowl; stir in yeast mixture. Turn dough onto lightly floured surface; knead about 15 minutes or until dough is smooth and elastic. Place dough in large oiled bowl, turning dough once to coat in oil. Cover; stand in warm place about 1 hour or until dough doubles in size.

3 Preheat oven to moderately hot.

4 Turn dough onto lightly floured surface; knead about 1 minute or until smooth. Divide dough into quarters; divide each quarter into five pieces.

5 Shape each piece into ball; place balls 5cm apart on two oiled oven trays. Cut small cross in top of each ball; spray lightly with oil. Cover loosely with plastic wrap; stand in warm place about 20 minutes or until dough doubles in size. (Can be refrigerated overnight at this stage. Stand at room temperature 1 hour before baking.) Bake, uncovered, in moderately hot oven about 15 minutes. Transfer to wire rack to cool.

makes 20
per roll 0.7g fat; 483kJ (115 cal)

brioche

PREPARATION TIME 40 MINUTES (PLUS STANDING TIME) **COOKING TIME** 15 MINUTES

One of the most popular French breads, brioche can be made in the shape of a loaf or roll. The most recognisable shape, however, is the delightful "brioche à tête", or brioche with a head, formed by placing a small ball of dough on top of a larger one. Some claim the word "brioche" originated because the bread was first baked in the town of Brie, while others believe the first brioche was kneaded incorporating brie cheese. Wherever or however it started, it's the best breakfast bread ever.

2½ cups (375g) plain flour
1½ teaspoons (5g) dried yeast
¼ teaspoon salt
¼ cup (55g) caster sugar
¾ cup (180ml) warm milk
5 egg yolks
125g butter
1 egg yolk, extra
2 teaspoons sugar

1 Combine flour, yeast and salt in large bowl. Combine caster sugar and milk in small jug; stir until sugar dissolves. Add milk mixture to flour mixture, then stir in egg yolks. Using wooden spoon, stir until mixture stiffens, then, using hand, mix until a firm dough forms.

2 Divide butter into 10 portions. Turn dough onto lightly floured surface; work each portion of butter into dough, kneading well after each addition, until all of the butter is incorporated and the dough is smooth and glossy. Place dough in lightly oiled large bowl, cover; stand in warm place about 2 hours or until dough doubles in size. (Can be refrigerated overnight at this stage.)

3 Grease 12 (⅓-cup/80ml) fluted ovenproof moulds or 12-hole (⅓-cup/80ml) muffin pan. Divide dough into 12 portions; remove about a quarter of each portion. Roll both the small and the large portions into balls. Place large balls in prepared moulds; make small indentation in top of each with fingertip, sit small round in each indentation. Brush each brioche with extra egg yolk; sprinkle with sugar. Stand, uncovered, in warm place about 1 hour or until dough doubles in size.

4 Meanwhile, preheat oven to moderate.

5 Bake brioche, uncovered, in moderate oven about 15 minutes. Serve warm.

makes 12
per brioche 12.3g fat; 1034kJ (247 cal)

Using wooden spoon, stir mixture until it starts to form a stiff dough.

Work butter into dough, kneading until dough is smooth and glossy.

With finger, make small indentation in which to sit the small round.

77

chocolate macadamia slice

PREPARATION TIME 15 MINUTES (PLUS REFRIGERATION TIME) **COOKING TIME** 5 MINUTES

200g butter
⅓ cup (115g) golden syrup
⅓ cup (35g) drinking chocolate
¼ cup (25g) cocoa powder
500g plain sweet biscuits, chopped finely
½ cup (75g) toasted macadamias, chopped coarsely
200g dark eating chocolate

1 Line 20cm x 30cm lamington pan with plastic wrap.
2 Combine butter, syrup, drinking chocolate and sifted cocoa in medium saucepan; stir over medium heat until mixture is smooth. Add biscuits and nuts; stir to combine.
3 Press mixture into prepared pan, cover; refrigerate until firm.
4 Stir chocolate in medium heatproof bowl over medium saucepan of simmering water until smooth. Spread chocolate over slice; refrigerate, uncovered, until firm. Cut into 4cm x 5cm pieces to serve.

makes 30
per piece 12.2g fat; 810kJ (194 cal)
tip Macadamias can be replaced with any other variety of nut.

mixed berry baked cheesecake

PREPARATION TIME 25 MINUTES (PLUS REFRIGERATION TIME) **COOKING TIME** 35 MINUTES

250g plain chocolate biscuits
125g butter, melted
2 x 250g packets cream cheese, softened
½ cup (110g) caster sugar
1 tablespoon lemon juice
2 eggs
⅓ cup (80g) sour cream
1 tablespoon plain flour
1½ cups (225g) frozen mixed berries, thawed

1 Grease and line 20cm x 30cm lamington pan.
2 Blend or process biscuits until mixture resembles fine breadcrumbs. Add butter; process until just combined. Using hand, press biscuit mixture into base of prepared pan, cover; refrigerate until firm.
3 Meanwhile, preheat oven to slow. Beat cheese, sugar and juice in large bowl with electric mixer until smooth. Add eggs, sour cream and flour; beat until combined. Spread cream cheese mixture over biscuit base; sprinkle with berries. Bake cheesecake, uncovered, in slow oven about 35 minutes. Cool to room temperature; refrigerate until firm.

serves 8
per serving 44.2g fat; 2431kJ (581 cal)
tip Use a hot knife to make cutting the cheesecake easier.

semolina slice

PREPARATION TIME 15 MINUTES (PLUS REFRIGERATION TIME) **COOKING TIME** 1 HOUR 50 MINUTES

Known variously throughout the Middle East and North Africa as basboosa, namoura or harisi, this sweet slice is saturated with a citrusy sugar syrup which gives it a lovely individual flavour.

1kg coarsely ground semolina
2½ cups (550g) sugar
1 cup (250ml) milk
125g butter
¼ cup (40g) blanched almonds

SUGAR SYRUP
3 cups (750ml) water
2 teaspoons lemon juice
1½ cups (330g) caster sugar
2 teaspoons orange flower water

1 Make sugar syrup.
2 Preheat oven to moderately slow. Grease 20cm x 30cm lamington pan.
3 Combine semolina and sugar in large bowl. Combine milk and butter in small saucepan; stir over low heat until butter melts. Pour into semolina mixture; stir to combine.
4 Spread mixture into prepared pan; smooth the top with a wet hand. Score slice into 4cm diamond shapes; centre one almond on each diamond. Bake, uncovered, in moderately slow oven about 1 hour 20 minutes or until slice is golden brown and slightly firm to the touch.
5 Cut through diamond shapes to bottom of slice; gradually pour cooled syrup over hot slice. Cool in pan.

SUGAR SYRUP Combine the water, juice and sugar in medium saucepan; bring to a boil. Reduce heat; simmer, uncovered, about 20 minutes or until syrup reduces to about 2½ cups. Cool to room temperature. Add orange flower water, cover; refrigerate 3 hours or overnight. (Syrup is best made the day before, covered and refrigerated; remove from refrigerator when slice goes into oven so that syrup is room temperature cool before pouring over hot slice.)

makes 28
per piece 5.2g fat; 1182kJ (282 cal)
tip Cover slice loosely with foil if slice starts to overbrown during cooking.

apple and rhubarb streusel slice

PREPARATION TIME 20 MINUTES (PLUS COOLING AND FREEZING TIMES) **COOKING TIME** 45 MINUTES

The German term for sprinkle, a streusel is great to have with tea or coffee mid-morning on a chilly weekend, and this one's rhubarb and apple filling gives it a wonderfully homely flavour. You need approximately 1kg of rhubarb for this recipe.

100g butter, softened
½ cup (110g) caster sugar
1 egg yolk
⅔ cup (100g) plain flour
¼ cup (35g) self-raising flour
1 tablespoon custard powder
4 cups (440g) coarsely
    chopped rhubarb
2 large granny smith apples
    (400g), sliced thinly
2 tablespoons honey
1½ teaspoons finely grated
    orange rind

STREUSEL
½ cup (75g) plain flour
¼ cup (35g) self-raising flour
⅓ cup (75g) firmly packed
    brown sugar
½ teaspoon ground cinnamon
80g butter, chopped

1 Make streusel.
2 Preheat oven to moderate. Line 20cm x 30cm lamington pan with baking paper, extending paper 3cm over long sides of pan.
3 Beat butter, sugar and yolk in small bowl with electric mixer until light and fluffy. Stir in combined sifted flours and custard powder. Using hand, press mixture into prepared pan. Bake, uncovered, in moderate oven about 20 minutes or until base is browned lightly. Cool slice for 15 minutes. Increase oven to moderately hot.
4 Meanwhile, cook rhubarb, apple, honey and rind in medium saucepan, stirring occasionally, about 6 minutes or until apples are just tender; cool 15 minutes. Spread over slice base; coarsely grate streusel over fruit. Bake, uncovered, in moderately hot oven about 15 minutes. Cool in pan before cutting.

STREUSEL Blend or process flours, sugar and cinnamon until combined. Add butter; process until ingredients just come together. Enclose in plastic wrap; freeze streusel about 1 hour or until firm.

serves 15
per serving 10.5g fat; 946kJ (226 cal)
tips The streusel mixture can be frozen for up to a week. The fruit mixture can be cooked and stored, covered, in the refrigerator overnight.

snickerdoodles

PREPARATION TIME 25 MINUTES (PLUS REFRIGERATION TIME) **COOKING TIME** 15 MINUTES

These amusingly named cookies have a cracked surface and are rolled in cinnamon sugar before being baked. There is dispute as to the true origin of the name (most often thought to be Dutch), but we know for certain that the biscuit translates as delicious.

250g butter, softened
1 teaspoon vanilla extract
½ cup (110g) firmly packed brown sugar
1 cup (220g) caster sugar
2 eggs
2¾ cups (410g) plain flour
1 teaspoon bicarbonate of soda
½ teaspoon ground nutmeg
1 tablespoon caster sugar, extra
2 teaspoons ground cinnamon

1 Beat butter, extract and sugars in small bowl with electric mixer until light and fluffy. Add eggs, one at a time, beating until just combined. Transfer to large bowl.
2 Stir combined sifted flour, soda and nutmeg, in two batches, into egg mixture. Cover; refrigerate dough 30 minutes.
3 Meanwhile, preheat oven to moderate.
4 Combine extra caster sugar and cinnamon in small shallow bowl. Roll level tablespoons of the dough into balls; roll balls in cinnamon sugar. Place balls on ungreased oven trays, 7cm apart; bake, uncovered, in moderate oven about 12 minutes. Cool biscuits on trays.

makes 50
per biscuit 4.4g fat; 390kJ (93 cal)

chocolate chip cookies

PREPARATION TIME 40 MINUTES (PLUS REFRIGERATION TIME) **COOKING TIME** 15 MINUTES

Originally called toll house cookies, these American biscuits were invented by the owner of the Toll House Inn, Ruth Graves Wakefield, in the 1930s in Massachusetts. Ruth added bits of dark chocolate to her favourite cookie dough, expecting them to melt during baking. Instead, the chocolate held its shape but became delicate and creamy – and the classic chocolate chip cookie was born!

250g butter, softened
1 teaspoon vanilla extract
¾ cup (165g) sugar
¾ cup (165g) firmly packed brown sugar
1 egg
2¼ cups (335g) plain flour
1 teaspoon bicarbonate of soda
2 cups (300g) dark chocolate Melts, chopped coarsely

1 Preheat oven to moderate.
2 Beat butter, extract, sugars and egg in small bowl with electric mixer until light and fluffy. Transfer to large bowl.
3 Stir combined sifted flour and soda, in two batches, into egg mixture. Stir in chocolate, cover; refrigerate 1 hour.
4 Roll level tablespoons of the dough into balls; place on greased oven trays 3cm apart. Bake, uncovered, in moderate oven about 12 minutes. Cool cookies on trays.

makes 40
per cookie 7.5g fat; 612kJ (146 cal)

refrigerator cookies

PREPARATION TIME 20 MINUTES (PLUS REFRIGERATION TIME) **COOKING TIME** 10 MINUTES

Freshly baked cookies in a matter of minutes! Keep this dough, rolled into a log shape and tightly sealed in plastic wrap, in your fridge for up to 3 days or in your freezer for up to 3 months. When a snack-attack strikes, just slice and bake. The frozen dough should be defrosted in the refrigerator before slicing and baking.

250g butter, softened
1 cup (160g) icing sugar mixture
2½ cups (375g) plain flour

1 Beat butter and sifted sugar in small bowl with electric mixer until light and fluffy. Transfer to large bowl.
2 Stir flour, in two batches, into butter mixture. Knead dough on lightly floured surface until smooth. Divide dough in half; roll each half into a 25cm log. Enclose in plastic wrap; refrigerate about 1 hour or until firm.
3 Meanwhile, preheat oven to moderate.
4 Cut rolls into 1cm slices; place on greased oven trays 2cm apart. Bake, uncovered, in moderate oven about 10 minutes or until browned lightly. Turn ccokies onto wire rack to cool.

makes 50
per cookie 4.2g fat; 313kJ (75 cal)
tip The thinner the slice, the crisper the cookie.

variations

VANILLA
Beat 1 teaspoon of vanilla extract into butter and sugar mixture.
per cookie 4.2g fat; 313kJ (75 cal)

CHOCOLATE AND HAZELNUT
Beat 2 tablespoons sifted cocoa powder into butter and sugar mixture, then stir in ⅓ cup hazelnut meal and ¼ cup finely chopped milk chocolate Bits before adding the flour. Bring back to room temperature before slicing.
per cookie 4.8g fat; 345kJ (82 cal)

LEMON
Beat 1 teaspoon finely grated lemon rind into butter and sugar mixture.
per cookie 4.2g fat; 313kJ (75 cal)

ORANGE
Beat 1 teaspoon finely grated orange rind into butter and sugar mixture.
per cookie 4.2g fat; 313kJ (75 cal)

Refrigerator cookie variations, from left: vanilla, chocolate and hazelnut, lemon, and orange.

cookies and cream cheesecake

PREPARATION TIME 20 MINUTES (PLUS REFRIGERATION TIME) COOKING TIME 5 MINUTES

The first recorded mention of cheesecake dates all the way back to Ancient Greece but it gained wide popularity in the Jewish delis of New York. Our version takes its flavour from the much-loved cookies and cream ice-cream variety.

250g plain chocolate biscuits
150g butter, melted
2 teaspoons gelatine
¼ cup (60ml) water
1½ cups (360g) packaged
    cream cheese, softened
300ml thickened cream
1 teaspoon vanilla extract
½ cup (110g) caster sugar
180g white eating
    chocolate, melted
150g cream-filled chocolate
    biscuits, quartered
50g dark eating chocolate, melted

1 Line base of 23cm springform tin with baking paper.

2 Blend or process plain chocolate biscuits until mixture resembles fine breadcrumbs. Add butter; process until just combined. Using hand, press biscuit mixture evenly over base and 3cm up side of prepared tin, cover; refrigerate 20 minutes.

3 Sprinkle gelatine over the water in small heatproof jug; stand jug in small saucepan of simmering water. Stir until gelatine dissolves; cool 5 minutes.

4 Beat cheese, cream, extract and sugar in medium bowl with electric mixer until smooth. Stir in gelatine mixture and white chocolate; fold in quartered biscuits. Pour cheesecake mixture over biscuit mixture in tin, cover; refrigerate about 3 hours or until set. Drizzle with dark chocolate to serve.

serves 12
per serving 42.7g fat; 2389kJ (571 cal)
tip Place the dark chocolate in a small plastic bag with the corner snipped off to help you drizzle the chocolate evenly over the cheesecake.

honey-coated pistachio and rosewater palmiers

PREPARATION TIME 30 MINUTES (PLUS REFRIGERATION TIME) COOKING TIME 15 MINUTES

Crisp and flaky French pastries, palmiers are so-named because they are folded and shaped to resemble the leafy arc formed by palm tree branches.

¾ cup (110g) toasted
  shelled pistachios
¼ cup (55g) caster sugar
2 teaspoons rosewater
½ teaspoon ground cinnamon
20g butter
2 tablespoons demerara sugar
2 sheets ready-rolled puff pastry
1 egg, beaten lightly
½ cup (175g) honey
1 teaspoon rosewater, extra

1 Blend or process nuts with sugar, rosewater, cinnamon and butter until mixture forms a coarse paste.

2 Sprinkle board with half of the demerara sugar; place one sheet of pastry on the sugar. Using rolling pin, press pastry gently into demerara sugar. Spread half of the nut mixture on pastry; fold two opposing sides of the pastry inwards to meet in the middle. Flatten folded pastry slightly; brush with a little of the egg. Fold each side in half to just meet in the middle; flatten slightly. Fold the two sides in half again so they just touch in the middle, flattening slightly. Repeat process with remaining demerara sugar, pastry sheet, nut mixture and egg. Enclose rolled pastry pieces, separately, with plastic wrap; refrigerate 30 minutes.

3 Meanwhile, preheat oven to moderately hot. Lightly grease two oven trays.

4 Cut rolled pastry pieces into 1cm slices; place slices flat on prepared trays about 1.5cm apart. Bake, uncovered, in moderately hot oven about 12 minutes or until palmiers are browned lightly both sides.

5 Meanwhile, combine honey and extra rosewater in small frying pan; bring to a boil. Reduce heat; simmer, uncovered, 3 minutes. Remove from heat.

6 Add hot palmiers, one at a time, to honey mixture, turning to coat all over; drain on greased wire rack. Serve cold.

makes 32
per palmier 4.5g fat; 382kJ (91 cal)

Use rolling pin to press one pastry sheet gently into demerara sugar.

Fold two sides of the pastry inwards to meet in the middle.

Fold each flattened half towards the middle again; flatten slightly.

dark chocolate and almond torte

PREPARATION TIME 20 MINUTES (PLUS STANDING TIME) COOKING TIME 55 MINUTES

Vienna almonds are whole almonds coated in toffee and are available from selected supermarkets, nut shops and gourmet food and specialty confectionery stores.

160g dark eating chocolate, chopped coarsely

160g unsalted butter

5 eggs, separated

¾ cup (165g) caster sugar

1 cup (125g) almond meal

⅔ cup (50g) toasted flaked almonds, chopped coarsely

⅓ cup (35g) coarsely grated dark eating chocolate

1 cup (140g) vienna almonds

DARK CHOCOLATE GANACHE

125g dark eating chocolate, chopped coarsely

⅓ cup (80ml) thickened cream

1 Preheat oven to moderate. Grease deep 22cm round cake pan; line the base and side with two layers of baking paper.

2 Stir chopped chocolate and butter in small saucepan over low heat until smooth; cool to room temperature.

3 Beat egg yolks and sugar in small bowl with electric mixer until thick and creamy. Transfer to large bowl; fold in chocolate mixture, almond meal, flaked almonds and grated chocolate.

4 Beat egg whites in small bowl with electric mixer until soft peaks form; fold into chocolate mixture, in two batches. Pour mixture into prepared pan; bake, uncovered, in moderate oven about 45 minutes. Stand cake in pan 15 minutes; turn cake, top-side up, onto wire rack to cool.

5 Meanwhile, make dark chocolate ganache.

6 Spread ganache over cake, decorate cake with vienna almonds; stand 30 minutes before serving.

DARK CHOCOLATE GANACHE Stir ingredients in small saucepan over low heat until smooth.

serves 14
per serving 30.8g fat; 1762kJ (421 cal)

Fold unbuttered section of dough over half of the buttered dough.

Cover surface of crème pâtissière completely with plastic wrap to prevent skin forming.

Brush dough around plum with egg mixture; bring opposite corners together, pinch gently.

danish pastries

PREPARATION TIME 1 HOUR 30 MINUTES (PLUS STANDING AND REFRIGERATION TIMES) COOKING TIME 25 MINUTES

1 cup (250ml) warm milk
¼ cup (55g) sugar
1 tablespoon (14g) dried yeast
20g butter, melted
1 egg, beaten lightly
2¼ cups (335g) plain flour
1 teaspoon salt
200g butter
825g can whole dark plums,
    drained, halved, seeded
1 egg, beaten lightly, extra
2 tablespoons milk
2 tablespoons water
⅓ cup (110g) apricot jam

CREME PATISSIERE
2 egg yolks
¼ cup (55g) sugar
2 tablespoons cornflour
¾ cup (180ml) milk
½ cup (125ml) cream
1 vanilla bean
30g butter

1 Whisk warm milk, sugar and yeast in medium jug until yeast dissolves, cover; stand in warm place about 15 minutes or until mixture is frothy. Stir melted butter and egg into yeast mixture. Sift flour and salt into large bowl; stir in yeast mixture, mix to a soft dough. Turn dough onto lightly floured surface; knead about 10 minutes or until dough is smooth. (Dough should be sticky.) Place dough in oiled large bowl, turning dough once to coat in oil. Cover with plastic wrap; stand at room temperature 1 hour. Refrigerate overnight.

2 Turn dough onto lightly floured surface; knead about 5 minutes or until smooth and elastic.

3 Roll dough into 25cm x 40cm rectangle, keeping corners square. Cut butter into small pieces; scatter half of the butter over two-thirds of the dough. Fold unbuttered section of dough over half of the buttered dough; fold remaining buttered section over it. With seam facing right, roll dough to form 25cm x 40cm rectangle again; fold one third of the dough onto centre third, fold remaining third on top. Enclose with plastic wrap; refrigerate 30 minutes.

4 Unwrap dough; with seam facing right, repeat step 3 with remaining butter.

5 Meanwhile, make crème pâtissière.

6 Unwrap dough; with seam facing right, repeat step 3 with no added butter.

7 Preheat oven to hot. Divide dough in half; roll each half into 30cm x 40cm rectangle. Cut each rectangle into 10cm squares; you will have 24 squares.

8 Centre 1 heaped teaspoon of the cold crème pâtissière on each square; top each with one plum half. Brush dough around plum with combined extra egg and milk; bring opposite corners together, pinch gently. Place pastries 5cm apart on ungreased oven trays; brush dough again with egg mixture. Bake, uncovered, in hot oven about 12 minutes or until browned lightly.

9 Meanwhile, combine the water and jam in small saucepan, stirring, over low heat until smooth; push jam mixture through sieve into small bowl. Brush pastries straight from the oven with jam mixture; transfer to wire rack to cool.

CREME PATISSIERE Whisk egg yolks, sugar and cornflour in medium bowl until light and fluffy. Combine milk and cream in medium saucepan. Split vanilla bean in half lengthways; scrape seeds into saucepan, then add pod. Bring mixture almost to a boil; discard pod. Whisking constantly, gradually pour milk mixture into egg mixture; return custard mixture to same saucepan. Cook over low heat, stirring constantly, until mixture boils and thickens; remove from heat. Return to same cleaned medium bowl with butter; stir until butter melts. Cover surface of crème pâtissière completely with plastic wrap to avoid skin forming; cool to room temperature. Crème pâtissière can be made a day ahead.

makes 24
per pastry 12.4g fat; 890kJ (213 cal)
tips Canned drained apricot halves or seeded cherries can be used instead of plums, if desired.
Pastry can be frozen (wrapped in plastic wrap) for up to 3 weeks.
Thaw, covered, at room temperature for 2 hours before rolling out.

quince and spice steamed pudding with orange syrup

PREPARATION TIME 25 MINUTES COOKING TIME 2 HOURS

Quince, a tart yellow-skinned fruit that turns a gorgeous coral pink when cooked, was
a symbol of love in Ancient Rome and was given to loved ones as a sign of commitment.

800g quinces
½ cup (125ml) water
1 tablespoon brown sugar
2 teaspoons finely grated
    orange rind
100g butter
½ cup (110g) firmly packed
    brown sugar, extra
2 eggs, beaten lightly
1½ cups (225g) self-raising flour
½ teaspoon bicarbonate of soda
2 teaspoons ground ginger
1 teaspoon mixed spice
½ cup (125ml) milk

ORANGE SYRUP
1 medium orange (240g)
1 cup (220g) caster sugar
1½ cups (375ml) water
6 cardamom pods, bruised
1 cinnamon stick
2 star anise

1 Peel quinces; cut into quarters. Using small knife, remove core; chop
coarsely. Place quince in large saucepan with the water, sugar and rind;
cook, covered, over low heat, stirring occasionally, about 30 minutes or
until quince softens. Cool to room temperature.

2 Beat butter and extra sugar in small bowl with electric mixer until light
and fluffy. Beat in eggs, one at a time, beating until combined between
additions. Stir in combined sifted flour, soda, ginger and spice until
smooth; stir in milk and cooled quince mixture.

3 Pour mixture into lightly greased 1.5-litre (6-cup) pudding steamer; cover
with tightly secured baking paper. Place pudding in large saucepan
with enough boiling water to come halfway up side of steamer; cover
saucepan with tight-fitting lid. Boil 1½ hours, replenishing pan with boiling
water as it evaporates.

4 Meanwhile, make orange syrup.

5 Turn pudding onto serving plate; pour half of the syrup over hot pudding.
Serve pudding accompanied with remaining syrup in a jug and a bowl of
whipped cream, if desired.

ORANGE SYRUP Using knife, cut rind from orange; cut rind into thin
strips. Squeeze juice from orange (you need ⅓ cup). Stir rind and juice in
small saucepan with remaining ingredients over low heat, without boiling,
until sugar dissolves. Reduce heat; simmer, uncovered, without stirring,
about 10 minutes or until syrup thickens slightly. Discard spices.

serves 8
per serving 12.7g fat; 1763kJ (421 cal)
tip Quinces can be substituted with pears or apples, if desired, reducing
cooking time accordingly.

apple and marmalade freeform pie

PREPARATION TIME 40 MINUTES (PLUS REFRIGERATION AND STANDING TIMES) **COOKING TIME** 1 HOUR 35 MINUTES

No need for a pie dish with this recipe. Freeform pies are not only easy to make but also result in a dessert with a beautifully rustic and homely appearance. You can use the remaining marmalade on slices of toasted ciabatta whenever you feel like it. Make the marmalade the day before you make the pie, if possible.

2½ cups (375g) plain flour
185g cold butter, chopped
2 egg yolks
½ cup (60g) finely grated
   cheddar cheese
¼ cup (60ml) water, approximately
6 medium apples (900g)
2 tablespoons water, extra
2 tablespoons brown sugar
2 teaspoons milk

CITRUS MARMALADE
1 small orange (180g)
1 medium lemon (140g)
1 tablespoon water
1½ cups (375ml) water, extra
2 cups (440g) caster sugar,
   approximately

1   Make citrus marmalade.
2   Process flour and butter until crumbly; add egg yolks, cheese and enough water to form a soft dough. Knead dough on lightly floured surface until smooth, cover; refrigerate 30 minutes.
3   Preheat oven to moderately hot.
4   Peel, core and halve apples; cut each half into six wedges. Cook apple with the extra water and sugar in medium saucepan, covered, stirring occasionally, about 5 minutes or until apple has just softened. Cool to room temperature.
5   Roll pastry between two sheets of baking paper to form 40cm circle. Remove top sheet of paper, turn pastry onto oven tray. Remove remaining sheet of baking paper.
6   Spread apple mixture over pastry, leaving a 5cm border. Dollop 6 rounded teaspoons of the marmalade onto apple mixture. Fold pastry up to partly enclose fruit; brush pastry evenly with milk. Bake, uncovered, in moderately hot oven about 30 minutes or until pastry is cooked and browned lightly. Dust with icing sugar, if desired, before serving.

CITRUS MARMALADE Cut orange and lemon in half; slice thinly. Remove seeds; place seeds in small bowl with the water, cover; stand overnight. Place fruit in medium microwave-safe bowl; cover with the extra water. Cover; stand overnight. Strain seed mixture into fruit mixture; discard seeds. Cook fruit mixture, covered, on MEDIUM (50%) in microwave oven, stirring every 5 minutes, about 30 minutes or until rind softens. Measure fruit mixture, then mix with equal measure of the caster sugar in same microwave-safe bowl. Cook, uncovered, on MEDIUM (50%) in microwave oven, stirring every 5 minutes, about 30 minutes or until marmalade jells when tested. Skim surface of marmalade; stand 10 minutes. Pour into hot sterilised jars, seal while hot. Makes 2 cups.

serves 6
per serving 31.6g fat; 3661kJ (875 cal)
tips Purchased marmalade can be used in this recipe.
To test if marmalade has jelled, dip a wooden spoon into marmalade, then hold spoon up with the bowl of the spoon facing you. When marmalade is ready, two or three drops will roll down the spoon and join in a heavy drop.

bread and butter pudding cake

PREPARATION TIME 40 MINUTES (PLUS STANDING AND COOLING TIMES) **COOKING TIME** 1 HOUR 20 MINUTES

While most bread and butter puddings call for stale bread, our modern take on this homely dessert calls for its own purpose-built sponge cake – which makes it especially delicious! Buy small brioche from the bakery section of your supermarket or from any French cake shop.

⅓ cup (55g) sultanas

⅓ cup (55g) raisins

⅓ cup (50g) coarsely chopped dried apricots

¼ cup (35g) dried currants

⅓ cup (65g) chopped dried figs

2 tablespoons mixed peel

¼ cup (60ml) brandy

2 tablespoons orange juice

2 small brioche (200g)

80g butter, melted

¼ cup (80g) apricot jam, warmed

1 tablespoon icing sugar mixture

SPONGE

4 eggs

½ cup (110g) caster sugar

¾ cup (110g) self-raising flour

50g butter, melted

CUSTARD

300ml thickened cream

1 cup (250ml) milk

2 eggs

4 egg yolks

½ cup (110g) caster sugar

1 Combine dried fruits, peel, brandy and juice in medium bowl, cover; stand overnight.

2 Preheat oven to moderately hot. Grease and flour deep 22cm round cake pan.

3 Make sponge. Make custard.

4 Grease same cleaned cake pan; line base and side with baking paper, extending paper 5cm above edge of pan. Cut each brioche vertically into six slices; brush slices on both sides with a quarter of the combined butter and jam.

5 Using serrated knife, split cake into three layers; place bottom layer in prepared pan, brush with another quarter of the jam mixture. Using 6cm cutter, cut eight rounds from middle layer; brush rounds on both sides with another quarter of the jam mixture, reserve.

6 Chop remaining cake layer coarsely. Layer half of the brioche then fruit mixture, chopped cake and remaining brioche slices in pan. Pour over remaining jam mixture. Pour hot custard over layered ingredients; top with reserved rounds. Bake, uncovered, in moderately slow oven 30 minutes. Cover with foil; bake in moderately slow oven about 30 minutes. Cool bread and butter pudding in pan 30 minutes; turn, top-side up, onto serving plate. Dust with sifted icing sugar.

SPONGE Beat eggs and sugar in small bowl with electric mixer until thick and creamy; transfer to large bowl. Gently fold in triple-sifted flour and butter. Pour mixture into prepared pan; bake, uncovered, in moderately hot oven about 20 minutes. Turn cake onto wire rack immediately to cool; decrease oven to moderately slow. (Can be made ahead to this stage. Cover; refrigerate overnight.)

CUSTARD Stir cream and milk in small saucepan over heat until almost boiling. Whisk eggs, yolks and sugar in large bowl. Whisking constantly, gradually add hot cream mixture to egg mixture; whisk until combined.

serves 12

per serving 25.6g fat; 2039kJ (487 cal)

tip You can use a purchased sponge cake, if you prefer.

orange syrup cake

PREPARATION TIME 25 MINUTES COOKING TIME 1 HOUR 10 MINUTES

1 large orange (300g)
2 cups (500ml) water
2 cups (440g) caster sugar
⅔ cup (160ml) brandy
250g unsalted butter, softened
1 cup (220g) caster sugar, extra
4 eggs
1½ cups (225g) self-raising flour
2 tablespoons cornflour

1 Preheat oven to moderately slow. Grease deep 22cm round cake pan; line base and side with baking paper.

2 Peel orange. Chop both the peel and the flesh of orange finely; discard seeds.

3 Stir flesh and peel in medium saucepan with the water, sugar and brandy over medium heat until sugar dissolves; bring to a boil. Reduce heat; simmer, uncovered, about 15 minutes or until orange skin is tender. Strain syrup into jug; reserve orange solids separately.

4 Beat butter and extra sugar in small bowl with electric mixer until light and fluffy. Add eggs, one at a time, beating until just combined between additions. Transfer mixture to large bowl.

5 Stir in combined sifted flour and cornflour, and reserved orange solids. Pour mixture into prepared pan; bake, uncovered, in moderately slow oven about 50 minutes.

6 Meanwhile, simmer reserved syrup over heat in small saucepan until thickened slightly.

7 Stand cake in pan 5 minutes, then turn, top-side up, onto wire rack set over tray. Pour hot syrup over hot cake; serve warm.

serves 12
per serving 19.1g fat; 2064kJ (493 cal)

chocolate mocha dacquoise terrine

PREPARATION TIME 20 MINUTES (PLUS REFRIGERATION TIME) **COOKING TIME** 45 MINUTES

A classic dacquoise is a layered meringue sandwiched with a butter-cream filling. It is served cold, often with a complementary seasonal fruit, or sometimes with nuts mixed into the butter cream.

4 egg whites
1 cup (220g) caster sugar
2 tablespoons cocoa powder
200g dark eating chocolate, chopped coarsely
¾ cup (180ml) cream
2 teaspoons cocoa powder, extra

MOCHA BUTTER CREAM
1 tablespoon instant coffee powder
2 tablespoons boiling water
100g unsalted butter
2¼ cups (360g) icing sugar mixture

1 Preheat oven to slow. Line each of three oven trays with baking paper; draw a 10cm x 25cm rectangle on each baking-paper-lined tray.
2 Beat egg whites in medium bowl with electric mixer until soft peaks form. Gradually add sugar, beating after each addition until sugar dissolves; fold in sifted cocoa.
3 Spread meringue mixture evenly over drawn rectangles; bake, uncovered, in slow oven about 45 minutes or until meringue is dry. Turn off oven; cool meringues in oven with door ajar.
4 Meanwhile, stir chocolate and cream in small saucepan over low heat until smooth, transfer to small bowl; refrigerate until firm. Beat chocolate mixture with electric mixer about 20 seconds or until just changed in colour.
5 Make mocha butter cream.
6 Place one meringue layer on serving plate; spread with half of the chocolate mixture, then top with half of the butter cream. Top with another meringue layer; spread with remaining chocolate mixture, then with remaining butter cream. Top with last meringue layer, cover; refrigerate 3 hours or overnight. To serve, dust with sifted extra cocoa powder.

MOCHA BUTTER CREAM Dissolve coffee powder with the boiling water in small bowl; cool 10 minutes. Beat butter in small bowl with electric mixer until pale in colour; gradually add sugar, beating until combined. Beat in coffee mixture.

serves 12
per serving 17.3g fat; 1649kJ (394 cal)

chocolate, pear and hazelnut self-saucing pudding

PREPARATION TIME 30 MINUTES COOKING TIME 1 HOUR 10 MINUTES

Frangelico, the Italian liqueur used in this recipe, is made from hazelnuts in an infusion of flowers and berries – and a glass of it perfectly complements this more-ish pudding.

100g dark eating chocolate, chopped coarsely
50g butter
⅔ cup (160ml) milk
¼ cup (25g) hazelnut meal
⅔ cup (100g) toasted hazelnuts, chopped coarsely
1 cup (220g) firmly packed brown sugar
1 cup (150g) self-raising flour
1 egg, beaten lightly
2 medium pears (460g)
300ml thickened cream
2 tablespoons icing sugar mixture
2 tablespoons Frangelico

FUDGE SAUCE
1¾ cups (430ml) water
100g butter
1 cup (220g) firmly packed brown sugar
½ cup (50g) cocoa powder, sifted

1 Preheat oven to moderate. Grease shallow 3-litre (12-cup) baking dish.
2 Stir chocolate, butter and milk in small saucepan over low heat until smooth. Transfer to large bowl; stir in hazelnut meal, nuts and brown sugar then flour and egg.
3 Peel and core pears; slice thinly. Place pear slices, slightly overlapping, in prepared dish; top with chocolate mixture.
4 Make fudge sauce; pour over chocolate mixture. Bake, uncovered, in moderate oven about 1 hour. Stand 10 minutes.
5 Meanwhile, beat cream, sugar and liqueur in small bowl with electric mixer until soft peaks form. Top pudding with Frangelico cream; serve warm.

FUDGE SAUCE Stir ingredients in small saucepan over low heat until smooth.

serves 6
per serving 60g fat; 4470kJ (1068 cal)
tip The Frangelico can be omitted from the whipped cream mixture for an alcohol-free dessert.

celebration cake

PREPARATION TIME I HOUR 30 MINUTES (PLUS REFRIGERATION TIME) COOKING TIME 2 HOURS I5 MINUTES

You'll feel like celebrating when you take the first bite out of this divine cake... chocolate mud cake, chocolate ganache, white chocolate custard and chocolate truffles... need we say more?

250g butter, chopped
200g dark eating chocolate,
    chopped coarsely
1½ cups (375ml) water
2 eggs
2 teaspoons vanilla extract
2 cups (440g) caster sugar
¾ cup (110g) self-raising flour
1¼ cups (185g) plain flour
¼ cup (25g) cocoa powder
50g white eating
    chocolate, melted

WHITE CHOCOLATE CUSTARD
¾ cup (180ml) milk
1 vanilla bean
2 egg yolks
1½ teaspoons gelatine
2 tablespoons water
130g white eating
    chocolate, melted
⅓ cup (80ml) thickened cream

CHOCOLATE TRUFFLES
75g dark eating chocolate
½ cup (125ml) thickened cream

CHOCOLATE GANACHE
200g dark eating chocolate,
    chopped coarsely
⅓ cup (80ml) thickened cream

1 Preheat oven to moderately slow. Grease deep 22cm round cake pan; line base and side with baking paper.

2 Stir butter, dark chocolate and the water in medium saucepan over low heat until smooth. Transfer mixture to large bowl; cool 10 minutes.

3 Meanwhile, beat eggs, extract and sugar in small bowl with electric mixer until thick and creamy; stir into chocolate mixture. Stir in sifted dry ingredients; pour batter into prepared pan. Bake, uncovered, in moderately slow oven about 1¾ hours. Stand cake in pan 10 minutes; turn cake onto wire rack to cool. Enclose cake with plastic wrap; refrigerate 3 hours or overnight.

4 Split cake horizontally a third of the way from the top. Place bottom two-thirds of cake on serving plate; using small teaspoon or melon baller, scoop about 14 deep holes (at equal distances apart and not through to bottom of cake) out of cake, reserving 1¼ cups of scooped-out cake pieces for truffles.

5 Make white chocolate custard; pour immediately into holes in cake. Replace top of cake, cover; refrigerate 2 hours.

6 Meanwhile, make truffles then chocolate ganache. Spread chocolate ganache over cake; decorate with truffles. Drizzle truffles with white chocolate; refrigerate 1 hour before serving.

WHITE CHOCOLATE CUSTARD Place milk in small saucepan. Split vanilla bean in half lengthways, scrape seeds into saucepan, then add pod; bring to a boil. Cool 10 minutes; discard pod. Whisk in egg yolks; transfer mixture to medium heatproof bowl. Place milk mixture over medium saucepan of simmering water, stir over heat about 10 minutes or until mixture thickens slightly and coats the back of a spoon. Sprinkle gelatine over the water in small heatproof jug; stand jug in same saucepan of simmering water. Stir until gelatine dissolves. Stir gelatine mixture into milk mixture, cover; cool 5 minutes. Add chocolate and cream; stir until smooth.

CHOCOLATE TRUFFLES Stir chocolate and cream in small saucepan over low heat until smooth. Stir in reserved scooped-out cake, cover; refrigerate until firm. Roll level teaspoons of the mixture into balls, place on trays, cover; refrigerate until firm.

CHOCOLATE GANACHE Stir ingredients in small saucepan over low heat until smooth.

serves 8
per serving 67.6g fat; 4910kJ (1173 cal)

Split cake horizontally a third of the way from the top.

Scoop deep holes out of cake using small spoon or melon baller.

Pour white chocolate custard immediately into holes of cake.

glossary

ALMOND flat, pointed-ended nut with pitted brown shell enclosing a creamy white kernel which is covered by a brown skin.

blanched brown skin removed.

flaked paper-thin slices.

meal also known as ground almonds; nuts are powdered to a coarse flour texture, for use in baking or as a thickening agent.

slivered small pieces cut lengthways.

vienna toffee-coated.

BACON RASHERS also known as slices of bacon, made from pork side, cured and smoked.

BAKING POWDER a raising agent consisting mainly of two parts cream of tartar to one part bicarbonate of soda (baking soda). The acid and alkaline combination, when moistened and heated, gives off carbon dioxide which aerates and lightens the mixture during baking.

BAMBOO SHOOTS the tender shoots of bamboo plants, available in cans; must be drained and rinsed before use.

BAVETTE long, flat pasta similar to linguine and tagliatelle; can be found at most supermarkets.

BAY LEAVES aromatic leaves from the bay tree used to flavour soups, stocks and casseroles.

BEAN SPROUTS also known as bean shoots; tender new growths of assorted beans and seeds germinated for consumption as sprouts.

BEEF some of the recipes in this book call for beef to be eaten raw. Buy the freshest beef available; it is always a good idea to check with your butcher if what you're purchasing can be eaten raw.

BEETROOT also known as red beets; firm, round root vegetable. Can be eaten raw, in salads; boiled and sliced; or roasted then mashed like potatoes.

BICARBONATE OF SODA alternatively known as baking soda.

BOK CHOY also called pak choi or chinese white cabbage; has a fresh, mild mustard taste and is good braised or in stir-fries. Baby bok choy is also available and is slightly more tender than bok choy.

BORLOTTI BEANS also known as roman beans, can be purchased fresh or dried. Borlotti can also be substituted for pinto beans because of the similarity in

BORLOTTI BEANS

appearance – both are pale pink or beige with darker red spots. They can be used for Mexican frijoles refritos (refried beans), and in soups and salads.

BREADCRUMBS

packaged fine-textured, crunchy, purchased, white breadcrumbs.

stale one- or two-day-old bread made into crumbs by grating, blending or processing.

BRIOCHE rich French yeast-risen bread made with butter and eggs. Available from pâtisseries or specialty bread shops.

BURGHUL also known as bulghur wheat; hulled steamed wheat kernels that, once dried, are crushed into various-sized grains. Used in Middle-Eastern dishes such as kibbeh and tabbouleh.

BUTTER use salted or unsalted ("sweet") butter; 125g is equal to one stick of butter.

BUTTERNUT PUMPKIN used interchangeably with the word squash, pumpkin is a member of the gourd family used either as one of many ingredients in a dish or eaten on its own. Various types can be substituted for one another. Butternut is pear-shaped with golden skin and orange flesh.

CAPERS the grey-green buds of a warm climate (usually Mediterranean) shrub, sold either dried and salted or pickled in a vinegar brine. Baby capers, those picked early, are very small, fuller-flavoured and more expensive than the full-sized ones. Capers, whether packed in brine or in salt, must be rinsed well before use.

CAPSICUM also known as bell pepper or, simply, pepper. Native to Central and South America, capsicums are sold red, green, yellow, orange or purplish black. Seeds and membranes should be discarded before use.

CARDAMOM native to India and used extensively in its cuisine; this spice can be purchased in pod, seed or ground form.

CAYENNE PEPPER a long, thin-fleshed, extremely hot red chilli; usually purchased dried and ground.

CHEESE

fetta Greek in origin; a crumbly textured goat or sheep milk cheese with a sharp, salty taste.

goat made from goat milk, has an earthy, strong taste; available in both soft and firm textures, in various shapes and sizes, sometimes rolled in ash or herbs.

gruyère a Swiss cheese having small holes and a nutty, slightly salty flavour.

parmesan a sharp-tasting, dry, hard cheese, made from skim or part-skim milk and aged for at least a year.

CHICKPEAS also called garbanzos, hummus or channa; an irregularly round, sandy-coloured legume used extensively in Mediterranean and Latin cooking.

CHILLI generally the smaller the chilli, the hotter it is. Use rubber gloves when seeding and chopping fresh chillies to prevent them from burning your skin.

chipotle also known as ahumado chillies, are jalapeño chillies which have been dried and smoked. Having a deeply intense smoky flavour rather than a blast of heat, chipotles average 6cm in length and are dark brown, almost black, in colour. They are available from herb and spice shops as well as many gourmet delicatessens.

flakes, dried deep-red dehydrated extremely fine slices and whole seeds; good for cooking or for sprinkling over already-cooked food.

powder made from ground chillies.

sauce, hot we used a hot Chinese variety made from bird's-eye chillies, salt and vinegar. Use sparingly, increasing the quantity to your taste.

sauce, sweet comparatively mild, Thai-type sauce made from red chillies, sugar, garlic and white wine vinegar.

thai red also known as "scuds", these chillies are small, medium hot, and bright red in colour.

CHINESE COOKING WINE
made from rice, wheat, sugar and salt, with 13.5% alcohol; available from Asian food stores. Mirin or sherry can be substituted.

CHOCOLATE

Choc Bits also known as chocolate chips or chocolate morsels; available in milk, white and dark chocolate. Made of cocoa liquor, cocoa butter, sugar and an emulsifier, these hold their shape in baking and are ideal for decorating.

drinking sweetened cocoa powder.

Melts are discs of compounded chocolate that are ideal for melting and moulding.

CLOVES dried flower buds of a tropical tree; can be used whole or in ground form. They have a distinctively pungent and "spicy" scent and flavour.

COCOA POWDER also known as cocoa; dried, unsweetened, roasted then ground cocoa beans.

COCONUT

cream available in cans and cartons; made from coconut and water.

milk not the juice found inside the fruit, which is known as coconut water, but the diluted liquid from the second pressing of the white meat of a mature coconut (the first pressing produces coconut cream).

Available in cans and cartons from supermarkets.

CORIANDER also known as cilantro or chinese parsley; bright-green-leafed herb with a pungent flavour. Also sold as seeds, whole or ground.

CORNFLOUR also known as cornstarch; used as a thickening agent in cooking.

COUSCOUS a fine, grain-like cereal product, originally from North Africa; made from semolina.

CREAM OF TARTAR the acid ingredient in baking powder; added to confectionery mixtures to help prevent sugar from crystallising. Keeps frostings creamy and improves volume when beating egg whites.

CUSTARD POWDER instant mixture used to make pouring custard; similar to North American instant pudding mixes.

EGG some recipes in this book call for raw or barely cooked eggs; exercise caution if there is a salmonella problem in your area.

EGGPLANT purple-skinned vegetable also known as aubergine. Can be purchased char-grilled in jars.

FENNEL also known as finocchio or anise; eaten raw in salads or braised or fried as a vegetable accompaniment. Also the name given to dried seeds having a licorice flavour.

FISH SAUCE also called nam pla or nuoc nam; made from pulverised salted fermented fish, most often anchovies. Has a pungent smell and strong taste; use sparingly.

FIVE-SPICE POWDER a fragrant mixture of ground cinnamon, cloves, star anise, sichuan pepper and fennel seeds.

FLAT-LEAF PARSLEY also known as continental parsley or italian parsley.

GALANGAL

GALANGAL the dried root of a plant of the ginger family. It is used as a flavouring, and is either removed before serving or left uneaten.

GELATINE we used powdered gelatine; also available in sheet form known as leaf gelatine.

GINGER also known as green or root ginger; the thick root of a tropical plant.

GOLDEN SYRUP is a by-product of refined sugar cane; pure maple syrup or honey can be substituted.

HAM HOCK is the lower portion of a hog's hind leg. It consists of the bone, flesh, fat and connective tissue. Usually smoked or cured, but also fresh, ham hocks are mainly used to flavour soups.

HARISSA Moroccan sauce or paste made from dried red chillies, garlic, oil and sometimes caraway seeds.

HOISIN SAUCE a thick, sweet and spicy Chinese paste made from salted fermented soy beans, onions and garlic; used as a marinade or baste, or to accent stir-fries and barbecued or roasted food.

HORSERADISH CREAM
a commercially prepared creamy paste made of grated horseradish, vinegar, oil and sugar.

JUNIPER BERRIES
the dried fruit from the evergreen tree of the same name; they give gin its distinctive flavour.

KAFFIR LIME LEAVES
aromatic leaves of a citrus tree bearing a wrinkled-skinned yellow-green

JUNIPER BERRIES

PEPITAS

fruit; used like bay leaves, especially in Thai cooking.

KALAMATA OLIVES small, sharp-tasting, brine-cured black olives.

KIPFLER POTATO small, finger-shaped, with a nutty flavour; great baked and in salads.

KITCHEN STRING made of a natural product such as cotton or hemp so that it neither affects the flavour of the food it's tied around nor melts when heated.

KUMARA Polynesian name of orange-fleshed sweet potato often confused with yam.

LEBANESE CUCUMBER short, slender and thin-skinned; also known as the european or burpless cucumber.

LEEK a member of the onion family, it resembles the green shallot but is much larger.

LEMON GRASS a tall grass smelling and tasting of lemon; the white lower part of each stem is used.

MASALA literally meaning blended spices; a masala can be whole spices, a paste or a powder, and can include herbs as well as spices and other seasonings. Traditional dishes are usually based on and named after particular masalas.

MINCE MEAT also known as ground meat.

MIXED PEEL candied citrus peel.

MIXED SPICE a blend of ground spices usually consisting of cinnamon, allspice and nutmeg.

MUSTARD

dijon a pale brown, distinctively flavoured, fairly mild mustard originally from Dijon, France.

seeds, black also known as brown mustard seeds; more pungent than the white (or yellow) seeds that are used in most prepared mustards.

OIL

olive made from ripe olives. Extra virgin and virgin are the most fully flavoured varieties.

peanut pressed from ground peanuts; most commonly used oil in Asian cooking because of its high smoke point, giving it the capacity to handle high heat without burning.

OYSTER SAUCE made from oysters and their brine, cooked with salt and soy sauce, then thickened.

PANCETTA cured pork belly; if unavailable, bacon can be substituted.

PAPRIKA ground, dried, red capsicum (bell pepper), available sweet or hot.

PEPITAS dried pumpkin seeds.

PIDE also known as turkish bread. Comes in long (about 45cm) flat loaves as well as individual rounds; made from wheat flour and sprinkled with sesame or black onion seeds.

PINE NUT this is not in fact a nut but a small, cream-coloured kernel from pine cones.

PISTACHIO pale green, delicately flavoured nut inside hard off-white shell. To peel, soak shelled nuts in boiling water for about 5 minutes; drain, then pat dry with absorbent paper. Rub skins with cloth to peel.

POLENTA a flour-like cereal made from ground corn (maize); alternatively known as cornmeal. Also the name of the dish made from it.

PRESERVED LEMON a North African specialty, the citrus is preserved, usually whole, in a mixture of salt and lemon juice. Can be rinsed and eaten as is, or added to casseroles and tagines to impart a rich salty-sour acidic flavour.

PROSCIUTTO cured, air-dried, pressed ham; usually sold thinly sliced.

QUINCE yellow-skinned fruit with hard texture and astringent, tart taste; eaten cooked or as a preserve.

RAISINS dried sweet grapes.

READY-ROLLED PUFF PASTRY packaged sheets of frozen puff pastry, available from supermarkets.

RICE

arborio small, round-grain rice well-suited to absorb a large amount of liquid.

basmati a white, fragrant long-grain rice. It should be washed several times before cooking.

jasmine a fragrant long-grain rice; white rice can be substituted but will not taste the same.

RICE PAPER There are two products sold as rice paper:

banh trang Vietnamese in origin, made from rice paste that's been stamped into rounds; can be kept at room temperature. Dipped briefly in water, these rounds become pliable wrappers for deep-fried or uncooked foods, most often vegetables.

glossy rice paper generally imported from Holland, whiter than banh trang, looks like a grainy sheet of paper. It is used in confectionery making and baking, and not eaten uncooked.

RICE STICK NOODLES also known as sen lek, ho fun or kway teow; popular South-East Asian dried rice noodles. Come in different widths – thin used in soups, wide in stir-fries – but all should be soaked in hot water until soft. Sen lek are the traditional noodles used in pad thai; before soaking they measure about 5mm in width.

ROCKET also known as arugula or rucola; a peppery-tasting green leaf which can be used in cooking or eaten raw in salad. Baby rocket leaves are smaller and less peppery.

ROSEWATER extract made from crushed rose petals and called gulab in India; used for its aromatic quality in many sweetmeats and desserts.

SAFFRON expensive spice that is the stigma of a crocus. Available in strands or ground form; imparts a yellow-orange colour to food.

SASHIMI fish sold as sashimi has met stringent guidelines regarding its treatment since leaving the water, however it is best to seek local advice from knowledgeable authorities before eating any raw fish.

SEMOLINA made from durum wheat milled into various-textured granules, all of these finer than flour. The main ingredient in good pastas, in some kinds of gnocchi and in many Middle-Eastern and Indian sweets.

SHALLOTS also called french shallots, golden shallots or eschalots; small, elongated, brown-skinned members of the onion family. Grow in tight clusters similarly to garlic.

SICHUAN PEPPER also known as szechuan or chinese pepper. Small, red-brown aromatic seeds resembling black peppercorns; have a peppery-lemon flavour.

SNAKE BEANS long (about 40cm), thin, round, fresh green beans, Asian in origin, with a taste similar to green or french beans. Used most frequently in stir-fries, they are also called yard-long beans because of their length.

SOY SAUCE made from fermented soy beans. Light soy sauce is light in colour but generally quite salty; there is a salt-reduced soy sauce available.

SPATCHCOCK a small chicken (poussin), no more than six weeks old, weighing a maximum 500g. Also, a cooking technique where a small chicken is split open, then flattened and grilled.

SPLIT PEAS also known as field peas; green or yellow pulses grown especially for drying, split in half along a centre seam. Used in soups, stews and, occasionally, spiced and cooked on their own.

SPRING ONION vegetable having a small, white walnut-sized bulb, long green leaves and narrow green-leafed tops.

STAR ANISE a dried star-shaped fruit of a tree native to China. The pods, which have an astringent aniseed or licorice flavour, are widely used in the Asian kitchen. Available whole or ground.

SUGAR we used coarse, granulated table sugar, also known as crystal sugar, unless otherwise specified.

brown an extremely soft, finely granulated sugar retaining molasses for its characteristic colour and flavour.

caster also known as superfine or finely granulated table sugar.

demerara small-grain golden crystal sugar.

icing mixture also known as confectioners' sugar or powdered sugar; pulverised granulated sugar crushed together with a small amount (about 3%) of cornflour added.

palm also known as nam tan pip, jaggery, jawa or gula melaka; made from the sap of sugar cane and palm trees. Light brown to black in colour and usually sold in rock-hard cakes; substitute it with brown sugar if unavailable.

pure icing also known as confectioners' sugar or powdered sugar.

SULTANAS also known as golden raisins; dried seedless white grapes.

SUMAC a purple-red, astringent spice that adds a tart, lemony flavour to foods; it is available from Middle-Eastern food stores and some supermarkets.

TAHINI a paste made from ground sesame seeds and used extensively in Middle-Eastern cooking, especially in sauces and dips.

TAMARIND CONCENTRATE the commercial distillation of tamarind pulp into a condensed, compacted paste. Used straight from the container, with no soaking or straining required, it can be diluted with water according to taste.

TOMATO

cherry also known as tiny tim or tom thumb tomatoes, small and round.

egg also called plum or roma, these are smallish and oval-shaped.

VIETNAMESE MINT

semi-dried partially dried tomato pieces in olive oil; softer and juicier than sun-dried, these are not a preserve and thus do not keep as long as sun-dried.

TURMERIC a member of the ginger family; a root that is dried and ground, resulting in the rich yellow powder used in most Asian cuisines. It is intensely pungent in taste but not hot.

VANILLA

bean dried, long, thin pod from a tropical golden orchid grown in Central and South America and Tahiti; the minuscule black seeds inside the bean are used to impart a luscious vanilla flavour in baking and desserts. A whole bean can be placed in the sugar container to make the vanilla sugar often called for in recipes.

essence obtained from vanilla beans infused in alcohol and water.

extract obtained from vanilla beans infused in water. A non-alcoholic version of essence.

VIETNAMESE MINT not in fact a mint at all, this narrow-leafed, pungent herb, also known as cambodian mint or laksa leaf (daun laksa), is widely used in many Asian soups and salads.

VINEGAR

balsamic authentic only from the province of Modena, Italy; it is made from a regional wine of white trebbiano grapes that are specially processed, then aged in antique wooden casks to give an exquisite pungent flavour.

malt this is made from fermented malt and beech shavings.

WATERCRESS one of the cress family, a large group of peppery greens used raw in salads, dips and sandwiches, or cooked in soups. It is highly perishable, so must be used as soon as possible after purchase.

WONTON WRAPPERS purchased in packages of 40 or more; made of flour and water. Gow gee and spring roll wrappers can be used as substitutes.

WORCESTERSHIRE SAUCE a thin, dark-brown spicy sauce used as a seasoning for meat, gravies and cocktails, and also as a condiment.

YOGURT we used unflavoured full-fat yogurt in our recipes unless stated otherwise.

ZUCCHINI also known as a courgette, this is a small green, yellow or white vegetable belonging to the squash family.

index

facts + figures

Wherever you live, you'll be able to use our recipes with the help of these easy-to-follow conversions. While these conversions are approximate only, the difference between an exact and the approximate conversion of various liquid and dry measures is minimal and will not affect your cooking results.

dry measures

metric	imperial
15g	½oz
30g	1oz
60g	2oz
90g	3oz
125g	4oz (¼lb)
155g	5oz
185g	6oz
220g	7oz
250g	8oz (½lb)
280g	9oz
315g	10oz
345g	11oz
375g	12oz (¾lb)
410g	13oz
440g	14oz
470g	15oz
500g	16oz (1lb)
750g	24oz (1½lb)
1kg	32oz (2lb)

liquid measures

metric	imperial
30ml	1 fluid oz
60ml	2 fluid oz
100ml	3 fluid oz
125ml	4 fluid oz
150ml	5 fluid oz (¼ pint/1 gill)
190ml	6 fluid oz
250ml	8 fluid oz
300ml	10 fluid oz (½ pint)
500ml	16 fluid oz
600ml	20 fluid oz (1 pint)
1000ml (1 litre)	1¾ pints

helpful measures

metric	imperial
3mm	⅛in
6mm	¼in
1cm	½in
2cm	¾in
2.5cm	1in
5cm	2in
6cm	2½in
8cm	3in
10cm	4in
13cm	5in
15cm	6in
18cm	7in
20cm	8in
23cm	9in
25cm	10in
28cm	11in
30cm	12in (1ft)

measuring equipment

The difference between one country's measuring cups and another's is, at most, within a 2 or 3 teaspoon variance. (For the record, one Australian metric measuring cup holds approximately 250ml.) The most accurate way of measuring dry ingredients is to weigh them. When measuring liquids, use a clear glass or plastic jug with the metric markings. (One Australian metric tablespoon holds 20ml; one Australian metric teaspoon holds 5ml.)

how to measure

When using graduated metric measuring cups, shake dry ingredients loosely into the appropriate cup. Do not tap the cup on a bench or tightly pack the ingredients unless directed to do so. Level top of measuring cups and measuring spoons with a knife. When measuring liquids, place a clear glass or plastic jug with metric markings on a flat surface to check accuracy at eye level.

Note: North America, NZ and the UK use 15ml tablespoons. All cup and spoon measurements are level.

We use large eggs having an average weight of 60g.

oven temperatures

These oven temperatures are only a guide. Always check the manufacturer's manual.

	°C (Celsius)	°F (Fahrenheit)	Gas Mark
Very slow	120	250	½
Slow	140 – 150	275 – 300	1 – 2
Moderately slow	170	325	3
Moderate	180 — 190	350 — 375	4 – 5
Moderately hot	200	400	6
Hot	220 — 230	425 — 450	7 – 8
Very hot	240	475	9

Are you missing some of the
world's favourite cookbooks?

The Australian Women's Weekly cookbooks are available from bookshops, cookshops, supermarkets and other stores all over the world. You can also buy direct from the publisher, using the order form below.

Title	RRP	Qty	Title	RRP	Qty
Almost Vegetarian	£5.99		French Food, New	£5.99	
Asian, Meals in Minutes	£5.99		Get Real, Make a Meal	£5.99	
Babies & Toddlers Good Food	£5.99		Good Food Fast	£5.99	
Barbecue Meals In Minutes (Sep 04)	£5.99		Great Beef Cookbook	£5.99	
Basic Cooking Class	£5.99		Great Chicken Cookbook	£5.99	
Beginners Cooking Class	£5.99		Great Lamb Cookbook	£5.99	
Beginners Simple Meals	£5.99		Greek Cooking Class	£5.99	
Beginners Thai	£5.99		Healthy Heart Cookbook	£5.99	
Best Ever Slimmers' Recipes	£5.99		Indian Cooking Class	£5.99	
Best Food	£5.99		Italian Cooking Class	£5.99	
Best Food Desserts	£5.99		Japanese Cooking Class	£5.99	
Best Food Mains	£5.99		Kids' Birthday Cakes	£5.99	
Big Book of Beautiful Biscuits	£5.99		Kids Cooking (Jul 04)	£5.99	
Biscuits & Slices	£5.99		Lean Food	£5.99	
Cakes & Slices Cookbook	£5.99		Low-fat Feasts	£5.99	
Cakes Cooking Class	£5.99		Low-fat Food For Life	£5.99	
Caribbean Cooking	£5.99		Low-fat Meals in Minutes	£5.99	
Casseroles	£5.99		Main Course Salads	£5.99	
Celebration Cakes	£5.99		Meals in Minutes	£5.99	
Chicken Meals in Minutes	£5.99		Mediterranean Cookbook	£5.99	
Chinese Cooking Class	£5.99		Middle Eastern Cooking Class	£5.99	
Christmas Book	£5.99		Midweek Meals in Minutes	£5.99	
Christmas Cooking (Nov 04)	£5.99		Muffins, Scones & Bread	£5.99	
Cocktails	£5.99		New Finger Food	£5.99	
Cooking for Crowds	£5.99		Pasta Cookbook	£5.99	
Cooking for Friends	£5.99		Pasta Meals in Minutes	£5.99	
Cooking For Two	£5.99		Potatoes	£5.99	
Creative Cooking on a Budget	£5.99		Quick Meals in Minutes	£5.99	
Dinner Beef	£5.99		Quick-mix Biscuits & Slices	£5.99	
Dinner Lamb (Apr 05)	£5.99		Quick-mix Cakes	£5.99	
Dinner Seafood	£5.99		Salads:Simple, Fast & Fresh	£5.99	
Easy Australian Style	£5.99		Saucery	£5.99	
Easy Curry	£5.99		Sensational Stir-Fries	£5.99	
Easy Spanish-Style	£5.99		Short-order Cook	£5.99	
Easy Vietnamese-Style	£5.99		Sweet Old Fashioned Favourites	£5.99	
Essential Barbecue	£5.99		Thai Cooking Class	£5.99	
Essential Microwave	£5.99		Vegetarian Meals in Minutes	£5.99	
Essential Soup	£5.99		Weekend Cook	£5.99	
Freezer, Meals from the	£5.99		Wicked Sweet Indulgences	£5.99	
French Cooking Class	£5.99		Wok, Meals in Minutes	£5.99	
			Total Cost:	£	

Mr/Mrs/Ms _____

Address _____

_____

Postcode _____ Country _____

Daytime phone ( ) _____

I enclose my cheque/money order

for £ _____

OR: please charge my

☐ Access ☐ Visa ☐ Mastercard

Cardholder's name _____

Card number

Expiry date ____ /____

Cardholder's signature _____

To order: Mail or fax — photocopy or complete the order form above, and send your credit card details or cheque payable to: Australian Consolidated Press (UK), Moulton Park Business Centre, Red House Road, Moulton Park, Northampton NN3 6AQ, phone (+44) (0) 1604 497531, fax (+44) (0) 1604 497533, e-mail books@acpuk.com

Non-UK residents: We accept the credit cards listed on the coupon, or cheques, drafts or International Money Orders payable in sterling and drawn on a UK bank. Credit card charges are at the exchange rate current at the time of payment.

Postage and packing: Within the UK, add £1.50 for one book or £3.00 for two books. There is no postal charge for orders of three or more books for delivery within the UK. For delivery outside the UK, please phone, fax or e-mail for a quote.

Offer ends 31.12.2004

Test Kitchen
Food director *Pamela Clark*
Food editor *Karen Hammial*
Assistant food editor *Amira Georgy*
Test Kitchen manager *Cathie Lonnie*
Home economists *Sammie Coryton,
Nancy Duran, Benjamin Haslam,
Elizabeth Macri, Christina Martignago,
Sharon Reeve, Susie Riggall,
Jessica Sly, Kirrily Smith, Kate Tait*
Editorial coordinator *Rebecca Steyns*
Nutritional information *Laila Ibram*

ACP Books
Editorial director *Susan Tomnay*
Creative director *Hieu Chi Nguyen*
Senior editor *Lynda Wilton*
Designer *Alison Windmill*
Studio manager *Caryl Wiggins*
Editorial/sales coordinator *Caroline Lowry*
Editorial assistant *Karen Lai*
Publishing manager (sales) *Brian Cearnes*
Publishing manager (rights & new projects)
 Jane Hazell
Brand manager *Donna Gianniotis*
Pre-press *Harry Palmer*
Production manager *Carol Currie*
Business manager *Seymour Cohen*
Assistant business analyst *Martin Howes*
Chief executive officer *John Alexander*
Group publisher *Pat Ingram*
Publisher *Sue Wannan*

Produced by ACP Books, Sydney.

Printed by Dai Nippon Printing in Korea.

Published by ACP Publishing Pty Limited, 54 Park St, Sydney; GPO Box 4088, Sydney, NSW 2001.
Ph: (02) 9282 8618 Fax: (02) 9267 9438.
acpbooks@acp.com.au
www.acpbooks.com.au
To order books, phone 136 116.
Send recipe enquiries to:
recipeenquiries@acp.com.au
AUSTRALIA: Distributed by Network Services, GPO Box 4088, Sydney, NSW 2001.
Ph: (02) 9282 8777 Fax: (02) 9264 3278.
UNITED KINGDOM: Distributed by Australian Consolidated Press (UK), Moulton Park Business Centre, Red House Rd, Moulton Park, Northampton, NN3 6AQ.
Ph: (01604) 497531 Fax: (01604) 497533
acpukltd@aol.com
CANADA: Distributed by Whitecap Books Ltd, 351 Lynn Ave, North Vancouver, BC, V7J 2C4.
Ph: (604) 980 9852 Fax: (604) 980 8197
customerservice@whitecap.ca
www.whitecap.ca
NEW ZEALAND: Distributed by Netlink Distribution Company, ACP Media Centre, Cnr Fanshawe and Beaumont Streets, Westhaven, Auckland.
PO Box 47906, Ponsonby, Auckland, NZ.
Ph: (09) 366 9966 ask@ndcnz.co.nz

Clark, Pamela.
The Australian Women's Weekly
The Weekend Cook.

Includes index.
ISBN 1 86396 359 6
1. Cookery. 2. Food. I. Title. II. Title: Weekend Cook. III. Title: Australian Women's Weekly.
641.5
© ACP Publishing Pty Limited 2004
ABN 18 053 273 546
This publication is copyright. No part of it may be reproduced or transmitted in any form without the written permission of the publishers.
First published 2004.

The publishers would like to thank the following for props used in photography:
Boxx Sydney, Surry Hills, NSW
Country Road HomeWear, stores nationally
Mud Australia, Marrickville, NSW.